"You are a political warrior"
🍁 Talk Show Host Charles Adler

"Nicholls is the outspoken, non-partisan ideologue who has been a thorn in the side of the federal conservatives since they started to move towards the political centre."
🍁 The Fraser Institute

"Gerry is a principled Canadian conservative and a brilliant strategist"
🍁 John McLaughlin, McLaughlin and Associates

"Gerry is the NCC's guardian of ideological purity"
🍁 David Somerville, former President
   of the National Citizens Coalition

"Gerry Nicholls was the brains behind the National Citizens Coalition."
🍁 Mike Duffy, host of *Mike Duffy Live*

"Gerry Nicholls is a brilliant wit and a principled conservative."
🍁 Paul Tuns, author/writer

"Gerry Nicholls is a fierce defender of democracy"
🍁 Linda Leatherdale, Business editor *Toronto Sun*

"Gerry Nicholls is a maverick, gadfly libertarian."
🍁 Michael Coren, host of the *Michael Coren Show*

"An important independent media commentator"
🍁 David Frum

ISBN 978-0-9732757-8-0

Cover Design by Michael Moon

Book Design by David Bolton

LOYAL TO THE CORE:
STEPHEN HARPER, ME AND THE NCC

GERRY NICHOLLS

FRE3DOM PRESS
CANADA INC.

FOR MY PARENTS

CONTENTS

I HAVE BEEN CALLED ONE OF THE TOP FIVE POLITICAL minds in the country.

Who called me that? OK, I did. But that's beside the point.

What matters is that for more than 20 years, I honed my political skills in the front line trenches in the never-ending fight for democratic freedoms and less government.

I was a soldier in the rough and tough political guerilla army known as the National Citizens Coalition.

It was a great place to work.

Not only was I helping to make Canada a better, freer country, but I had the pleasure of knowing my work was upsetting the country's left-wing élite.

What's more, I had a chance to work with a lot of interesting people, including a guy who eventually went on to become the Prime Minister of Canada.

Yes, that's right. I'm talking about Stephen Harper, who from 1998 until 2001 was president of the National Citizens Coalition.

You don't hear Harper talk much about his stint at the NCC. In fact, he never talks about it at all.

He never mentions it during media interviews. Even his official Conservative Party biography sort of skips over it.

Mind you, I can understand why Harper is reticent to discuss his NCC past.

After all, his media and political opponents on the left like to make a big deal about his former job.

Usually, they invoke the NCC when trying to convince Canadians that Harper has some sort of scary "hidden agenda." They say stuff like, "If you want to really know what the prime minister will do should he win a majority government, just remember he used to lead the big, bad NCC."

To add to the scaremongering, they inevitably describe the NCC as "extreme right-wing" or "radical right-wing" or "ultra right-wing" or "ultra-radical extreme right-wing."

Of course, that kind of nonsense is not fair to the NCC or to Stephen Harper.

The NCC is and always has been a mainstream organization. After all, what's radical about pushing for lower taxes, wanting a stronger defence, fighting for free political expression and for the rights of unionized employees?

Those are the kind of things Stephen Harper fought for during his time at the NCC.

Unfortunately, you don't hear that side of the story from the media.

That's why I wanted to write this book. I simply wanted to set the record straight about Stephen Harper, me and the NCC.

Certainly, somebody had to write down the history of a remarkable organization like the National Citizens Coalition, if for no other reason than to offset the anti-NCC, left-wing propaganda that's floating around out there.

The NCC is unique. It is not a think tank or a "single-issue" advocacy organization or a lobby group. Yet the NCC has, over the years, waged magnificent campaigns to expose government waste, to protect democratic rights and to provide a voice for thousands of Canadians who believe less government is better than more government.

Besides providing a mini-history, I wanted to brag a bit about the NCC's creative work, especially its punchy, take-no-prisoners ad campaigns. Our billboards, our TV spots, our radio commercials were not only hard-hitting and effective but they often featured something that's sadly lacking in political discourse these days: a sense of fun.

And a large chunk of this book is about my relationship with my old boss, Stephen Harper. I want Canadians to know how Stephen Harper the politician differs from Stephen Harper the NCC president.

The Stephen Harper of today is cold, unemotional and detached. Whereas the Stephen Harper I knew was … well, he was cold and unemotional and detached then too. But he was also a man committed to ideological conservatism.

Somewhere along the line, after he became leader of the Conservative Party, Stephen changed. Simply put, he sold his ideological soul to the devil of political expediency. And in the process, the NCC, which had become entangled in Stephen's ambition, lost a bit of its soul too. For a while, so did I.

So this book is also a warning to other conservative groups. If you see a partisan politician heading in your direction, turn around and run as fast as you can in the other direction.

Finally, this book is a kind of therapy for me. Not long ago, the NCC fired me without warning and without explanation. It was tough. It hurt. After I lost my job, my life seemed empty and incomplete. Admittedly, part of it was bitterness, a sense of betrayal. But it was also something more, something deeper. For lack of a better term, it was a lack of closure.

I never got a chance to properly say goodbye to NCC supporters, to the people who had fought with me side by side, in so many battles, over so many years.

So if you are an NCC supporter, past or present, this book is also my way of saying thank you for being there when your country needed you.

CHAPTER 1
THE CONTRARIAN

On April 5th, 2007, my name was splashed all over the media. The *Toronto Star*, the *Globe and Mail* and the *National Post* all had articles about me.

Now ordinarily that kind of publicity would have made me a really happy guy.

But this time it made me sick.

That's because those newspaper articles sported headlines like "Harper Critic Loses Lobby Group Job," and "Citizens Coalition Official says he was fired" and "Vice-President of group promoting free enterprise let go after 22 years."

The "Harper Critic" and "Citizens Coalition Official" were me. I was making news because I had been fired. That's not the kind of thing you like to read with your morning coffee.

The job I had been fired from – on April 4th, 2007 – was Vice President of the National Citizens Coalition, a pro-free market advocacy group known for its aggressive media campaigns and for the fact that Stephen Harper was its president before he became Prime Minister of Canada.

In fact, it was Stephen who promoted me to the post of vice president, a position which basically put me in charge of the NCC's communications and political strategy. Overall, I had been in the employ of the NCC for more than 20 years.

So to be told after all that time that I wasn't wanted anymore really hurt. Of course, getting fired isn't fun for anybody. But for me, losing my job at the NCC was traumatic beyond belief. I was not just hurt or angered, I was devastated. I was shocked. I was stunned. You have to understand that for me the NCC was not just a job, not just a place where I put in eight hours a day. It was much more than that. It was my life. It was my identity. The NCC helped make me who I was, and I helped make the NCC what it was – Canada's leading organization for the defence of economic and political freedoms.

I gave the organization everything I had to give. I happily worked weekends. Typically, I showed up at the office before 7:30 AM and usually left much later than 5:00 PM. It was hard work, but I enjoyed it and I firmly believed in the group's mission of promoting "more freedom through less government."

This may sound corny, but working at the NCC gave me a sense that I was helping to make a difference in this country, that I was helping to make Canada a freer and better place.

Do I sound bitter? Maybe I am. And maybe this all sounds a little melodramatic. I suppose it was naïve to pour myself into my job to such a degree or to expect that my loyalty to the organization would be reciprocated with loyalty to me. For some reason I believed the NCC was a different sort of workplace, more like a family.

Turns out I was wrong. But hey, life doesn't always work out the way you want. Somehow the NCC will just have to get along without me – and me without it. And besides, it's not as if I grew up believing my destiny was to be a champion for right-wing ideology.

Indeed, I was born and grew up in Windsor, Ontario, car capital of Canada and a bastion of liberalism and union boss socialism. My father, a house painter by profession, was of English-Scottish-Irish heritage, while my mother was pure laine French-Canadian, making me, I suppose, as typically Canadian as you can get. We didn't talk a lot about politics in my family. When it came to voting we always supported the Liberal Party because ... well, because we were Catholics and Catholics always voted that way. I am not sure but I suspect there is some catechism somewhere which instructs Catholics along the lines of "Thou Shalt Always Vote Liberal." The Progressive Conservatives, on the other hand, was the party for Protestants and the NDP was the party for heretics.

That's not to say we were believers in all the stuff usually associated with big "L" liberalism, like big government, massive social programs and coddling criminals. Far from it. We were more like social conservatives, staunch believers in traditional family values, law and order and most of all in anti-communism. (Communists were atheists and therefore automatically evil.) For light reading my grandmother used to send me pamphlets outlining all sorts of communist atrocities that were taking place in various third world countries, usually involving the torture of some Catholic missionary or the burning down of churches.

As for me, I was not all that political in my early years. Or at least I didn't know much about political philosophies or ideas. My interest was history, more specifically military history. But I did have a bit of a contrarian streak in me which caused me to rebel against the family's overall conservative stance. To get a reaction I would sometimes express sympathy for the Soviet Union, explaining in a smug teenage know-it-all sort of way that its policies weren't all that bad or that its "evilness" was exaggerated. And I also began to adopt typical nationalistic Canadian attitudes which led me to embrace anti-Americanism, which in turn led me to flirt with the notion of supporting the NDP.

My political attitudes started to change in 1977 when I enrolled at the University of Windsor. While at university, where I pursued a degree in International Relations, I found myself surrounded by left-wing professors and students.

And by left-wing I mean bona fide Communists, Marxists and even Trotskyites. Grandma would have been mortified. Even the campus priest was a leftie, who preached what I came to call the "Gospel According to Marx." Once again, my contrarian nature kicked in. I didn't want to be like all the lefties. I wanted to be different. And the best way to be different was to be a conservative.

It was around that time that I started to read magazines like *National Review*, and books like Barry Goldwater's *Conscience of a Conservative* and Alexis de Tocqueville's *Democracy in America*. And the more I read, the more I found something about conservatism just made sense. Whereas left-wing thought was based on emotion, conservatism was based on reason. Something about that appealed to me. It just felt right.

What I also found appealing about conservatism was its emphasis on individual freedom. I never liked it when people told me how to act or how to think. And I came to see socialism as basically a bunch of politicians, bureaucrats and other authority figures telling me how to run my life, as if they knew what was best for me. The more I read and studied, the more it seemed obvious that conservatism with its emphasis on free market capitalism and individualism was the only political philosophy consistent with individual freedom.

So, armed with the intellectual ammunition provided by people like William F. Buckley and Milton Friedman, I started to challenge professors and to debate other students.

I loved the ensuing political combat. Nothing made me happier than getting under the skin of the Left. So much did I enjoy riling the left-wing faculty that when it came time to write my MA history thesis, I decided to write a defence of the most notorious right-winger of them all – the Wisconsin Red-Baiter Senator Joseph McCarthy. That caught people's attention, let me tell you.

Still even though I was becoming much more politically-inclined, my true love was still history and I was hoping to continue my studies in that area. But my thesis advisor poured cold water on my dreams, explaining there were no jobs out there for people with PhDs in history.

My next idea was to get a job with Canada's Foreign Service. As a first step toward that goal I took an exam on campus with about 300 other aspiring diplomats. And I guess I did pretty well because I was one of only four students invited to take part in a special job interview with three representatives from the Foreign Service. At first the interview went great. I confidently fielded all their questions about Canada's history and current international events. But then disaster struck. One of the interviewers asked, "What do you think of the government's National Energy Program?" Without hesitation I answered, "I think it's pure economic stupidity." Given that the interviewers were probably all Liberals, it wasn't exactly a diplomatic answer. In fact, the interviewer who asked the question made a little note on a pad of paper. I didn't see what he wrote but I was pretty certain it was something like, "I would rather eat glass than hire this guy." Needless to say,

I didn't get called back for any future interviews.

After that fiasco, I figured my future might be in journalism or maybe in public relations, where I could help oil companies and other huge multinational corporations in their quest to exploit the masses. So in 1983 I enrolled in the University of Western Ontario's graduate journalism program, where I managed to earn an MA.

After graduating from Western in 1984, I moved back to Windsor. There, I got involved in the campaign of a local PC candidate named Tom Porter who was running in that year's federal election. I did this realizing full well that Tories had about as much success winning elections in Windsor as General Custer had fighting Indians.

Essentially, my job was to be Porter's executive assistant, which meant that I tagged along on his door-knocking forays and kept track of the reaction he elicited at each doorstep. After each visit I jotted down on a clipboard whether the people at the door were leaning Tory, leaning Liberal or whether they chased us away with a meat cleaver. I also volunteered to go canvassing on my own in parts of the riding where few Tories had the courage to enter, hard-core working-class neighborhoods. And, yes, strolling through those streets wearing a blue T-Shirt emblazoned with the words "Porter Supporter" and the PC logo was sometimes a challenge. But I survived.

On election night, as the campaign team and other supporters gathered in our office to watch the returns, I thought we actually had a good chance to win. And indeed, our dreams seemed to come true when at about 8:30 PM the Windsor CBC news affiliate announced Porter had pulled out an upset victory. The whole place erupted in cheers. Porter was ecstatic and promised me a job in Ottawa. But our joy lasted for approximately five minutes. Turns out the CBC had made a mistake; somebody at the station had misread the returns. Porter had actually lost, finishing a close second to the NDP candidate Howard McCurdy. Oops.

After that, the local Tories were keen to keep me involved in the riding association and offered me some sort of title or other, but I had a job waiting for me back at the University of Western Ontario. So I headed back to London in the fall. It wasn't all that much of a job. I was working for something called Westex News, which was a project operated out of the School of Journalism. My job was to take agricultural news from the Canadian Press wire and from other sources, re-write it into small bite-sized stories and then transmit them via computer to farmers who would subscribe to our service. It was actually an idea way ahead of its time. Unfortunately, it was probably too far ahead of its time. After about a year, the project's funding ran out and I was out of a job.

Luckily for me, however, Peter Desbarats, the Dean of Journalism at Western, suggested I contact Colin M. Brown, the president of the conservative advocacy group the National Citizens Coalition. Desbarats, who knew of my political leanings, told me the NCC was looking for somebody with a journalistic background. I liked the idea. I was, by that time, a big fan of the NCC, having joined the group as a member in 1982. I joined because the NCC was one of the few Canadian-based organizations that actually promoted a brand of pure conservatism. Unlike the federal PC party, which leaned too far to the left for my taste, the NCC was unabashedly against socialism and unflinchingly pro-free market.

I contacted the NCC and arranged an interview with the group's vice president, a man named David Somerville. We met in a pub across the street from the NCC office and chatted about politics and political philosophy and about the NCC for about an hour. Before I left, I asked David how many other people were applying for the job and he said, basically, "You're it." I figured I had the job in the bag.

But my confidence started to waver after a week had gone by without any word from the NCC. Did I have the job or not? Finally I decided to take the initiative and called up the NCC to get the lowdown. A man answered the phone. It was Colin M. Brown. "Hi Mr. Brown," I said a little nervously. "It's Gerry Nicholls here. I interviewed for a job with the NCC about a week ago. I was just wondering if I got the job?"

There was a pause at the other end of the phone. And then Colin said, "Yes, you have the job. But do you really want it? It only pays $15,000 a year." Since I was earning approximately 0 dollars a year, $15,000 sounded like a good salary. "Yes" I exclaimed. "I want the job!" So that was it. I was officially working for the National Citizens Coalition, meaning not only could I engage in my favorite pastime of left-wing baiting, but now I would actually get paid for it. My career in the wacky world of politics was about to begin.

CHAPTER 2
A HOBBY THAT WENT BERSERK

I STARTED MY NCC JOB ON JULY 15TH, 1985, ONE DAY after my 27th birthday. Back then the NCC office was located in a downtown Toronto office building. It had a charming look about it from the outside, with its quaint Art Deco architecture and its Group of Seven mural over the entrance., On the inside, however, the building wasn't so much charming as it was old and tired. As for the NCC suite, well it was hardly lavish. The carpeting was worn and ugly, the walls desperately needed a paint job and the chairs and desks looked like rejects from the Salvation Army. In keeping with the NCC's austere surroundings, my "office" – which also doubled as the NCC storeroom – featured a rickety wooden straight back chair, an even more rickety table and an ancient typewriter. All of this didn't really jibe with what I had read about the NCC being an organization "for the rich."

However, I soon discovered the NCC actually was rich, but its true wealth was its staff, the people who worked there. People like Colin M. Brown, the NCC's founder and first president. One of Canada's leading life insurance salesmen, Colin was the kind of guy who liked to get involved to help his community. He raised money for charities; he organized student exchanges between Ontario and Quebec to help promote national unity; he even set up a "Turn in a Pusher" program to help fight drug crime. Simply put, Colin was a man who, when he saw something was wrong, did everything he could to make it right. And by the late 1960s, Colin believed many things were going wrong in his beloved country. Those were the days when Lester Pearson and Pierre Trudeau were in the early stages of unleashing a revolution that would transform Canada into the bloated welfare state we know today. The trendy opinion at the time was that bigger government was better government. But Colin didn't buy it. He had the wisdom to foresee that the Trudeau revolution would ultimately lead to nothing but high taxes, massive debt and less freedom.

Yet at the time, nobody was ringing the alarm bell. Our entire political and media establishment seemed to be singing from the same left-wing hymn book. In other words, a political vacuum existed in Canada. No organization, no political party was speaking out for freedom and for Canada's traditional values. Colin decided to change that. Always a fighter, this World War II vet took up his sword and declared war on Trudeau's socialist vision.

In 1967, using his own money, he bought a full-page newspaper ad to warn Canadians about the dangers of the rapidly escalating size of government. The ad declared, "All federal parties, in their race for votes seem prepared to make Canadians, in all walks of life, the heaviest taxed people in the world." At the end of the ad, Colin included this simple request, "If you share my alarm, your support is welcome."

Of course, attacking big government in those days wasn't exactly a way to win friends. But Colin didn't care. As his friend Ken McDonald would later write about him, Colin ..."was the reverse of a political compromiser: he was guided by principle, loved his country, had an abiding faith in ordinary people, in their decency and goodwill, and was always ready to take on the principalities and powers that oppressed them."[1]

It was ordinary people who responded to his message. After that first newspaper ad appeared, hundreds of people wrote back to this man who was speaking out for freedom. They thanked him for having the courage to take a stand and, just as importantly, they sent him money so he could publish more newspaper ads. And encouraged by the enthusiastic response, that's exactly what Colin did. Over the next few years he placed more newspaper ads, ads he wrote himself in the basement of his London, Ontario home, ads which attacked socialized healthcare, the Post Office monopoly and government waste.

These ads were unpolished, with headlines like, "This year, increased government spending will cost your family $589.06 extra," but their bluntness had a raw power that mobilized people. More importantly, Colin was providing a voice for Canadians who didn't buy into Trudeau's big government dreams and who had no one else to speak for them. These Canadians saw in Colin a man who had the courage of his convictions, a man who was saying the things they longed to hear, a man who wasn't afraid to stand up for what was right. And so the grassroots support for his message continued to grow. As his son later recalled, letters to his father "were now piling up at the London post office (the Postmaster appeared at his door one day hopping mad), in his London Life office, in the trunk of his car and in Uncle Jim Kenny's Ottawa basement."[2] It was an amazing phenomenon; Colin called it a "hobby that went berserk."

By the mid 1970's, his "hobby" became so demanding of his time that he decided he could no longer operate it as a one man band. So in 1975, using seed money from business associates and friends, Colin created "The National Citizens' Coalition" – a non-profit corporation with an office in Toronto and a full-time paid staff.

The newly-minted NCC announced itself, naturally, with a full-page newspaper ad, proclaiming itself an organization for people who thought "politicians and union bosses didn't have all the answers." The Citizens' Coalition, explained the ad, "is a non-partisan body of Canadians … who would otherwise have no group representation of their views on the way we are governed." And so the NCC was born, with the motto "more freedom through less government."

Before long, this brash new organization began to make waves. The NCC strategy in those days was simple: push

20

conservative messages by placing ads in major newspapers. These ads served multiple purposes: they got the word out, they generated revenue for the NCC, they recruited new supporters and they made life difficult for MPs. Indeed, it wasn't uncommon for MPs to find a mountain of protest mail on their desks whenever the NCC ran an ad campaign. In 1981, for instance, the NCC ran an ad campaign against the Liberal government's plans to boost taxes, which generated such a groundswell of protest that in the words of left-wing journalist Brooke Jeffrey it "undoubtedly contributed to the withdrawal of the MacEachen budget."[3]

Unfortunately, I didn't have the chance to work with Colin for long, as he died in 1987 at the age of 73. But the time I did work for him was special. I was impressed not only by his commitment to freedom, but by his honesty, his generosity, his courage and by his quiet brand of confident leadership. He was a man of honour who never, ever backed down from a fight. After he died, I made it my goal to ensure the NCC would always live up to his great legacy.

Colin's successor as NCC president was David Somerville. He had been with the organization since the late 1970s, first as a researcher then as the group's vice president. Before that he had worked as a reporter for the *Toronto Sun* and was the author of *Trudeau Revealed*, a book exposing Pierre Trudeau's hard left political views. Like Colin, David was a scrapper. With his Clark Kent-style glasses, his closely cropped hair and his moustache he was an intense looking man. And this was one case where you could definitely judge a book by its cover – David was intense– a rock-ribbed, dyed-in-the-wool, hard right-wing, ideological conservative. He was a political pit bull, who relished sinking his teeth into the left's sacred cows. To David, politics was war. The enemy was Trudeau-style socialism and he knew only one strategy – attack, attack, attack. As he once put it, "If you want red meat for breakfast then you want to get involved in something like the National Citizens Coalition."[4] Under his leadership the NCC became much more of an aggressive, "in your face" style organization.

The NCC also had help from Arthur Finkelstein, a professional American political consultant and pollster. Colin Brown had hired Arthur to provide the NCC with advice and guidance and it was the best decision he ever made. Simply put, Arthur is a political genius and a masterful strategist. He had masterminded successful campaigns for such Republican luminaries as Ronald Reagan, Al D'Amato, Jessie Helms and George Pataki. In fact, at the time he worked with us (which was from 1982 to 1996), Arthur had been in charge of twenty-four successful Senate campaigns, more than any other consultant in American history.[5] He also ran several successful campaigns in Israel, helping to elect people like Benjamin Netanyahu. Arthur's success stemmed from his innovative polling techniques and from astute messaging. He also pioneered a hard-edged style of campaigning, more or less perfecting the attack ad as an effective political weapon. His greatest claim to fame in the 1990s was that he almost single-handedly made the term "liberal" a dirty word in the American political lexicon, with ads like this: "*That's liberal. That's Jack Reed. That's wrong. Call liberal Jack Reed and tell him his record on welfare is just too liberal for you.*"

Why did a big-time successful consultant like Arthur decide to work for a small Canadian group like the NCC? He did it because, unlike other political consultants, Arthur was not a hired gun. An ardent libertarian, he only chose as his clients people and organizations who actually believed in conservatism. That's why he worked for us. He believed in what we were trying to do in Canada. Plus, I think he just enjoyed being associated with an organization that was ideologically pure and that never compromised its values.

And Arthur was quite a character. He spoke in a broad Brooklyn accent, never wore a tie, had a fondness for onion rings and liked to kick off his shoes and parade around the room while dispensing anecdotes and political advice in equal measure. But he was also a stern and demanding taskmaster. He had little patience for either incompetence or laziness, much to my chagrin. Many a time, I emerged from an "Arthur meeting" shaking and distraught. What I didn't appreciate at the time was that Arthur was pushing me to get better and tougher. Over the years, as my own competence and confidence grew, Arthur became less of a consultant to me and more of a mentor. Finally, he became a friend. It was Arthur who taught me everything I know about political strategy and communication. He taught me, for instance, that politics was not an intellectual exercise, but a blood sport. Once you found a weakness in your enemy, you had to exploit it without mercy. If that meant using attack ads or going negative, so be it. He also ingrained in me the idea that good political messages were simple and repetitive. The way Arthur saw it, if you couldn't get your message across in a 15 second radio ad or paste it on a billboard, you were doing something wrong. But the most important thing I learned from Arthur was the importance of sticking by your principles. Arthur firmly believed that conservative politicians did not have to compromise their ideals for the sake of winning elections. He believed that with a proper communication strategy based on sound polling, principled conservatives could win. Indeed, this was something he had proven time and time again with his own candidates, who were often elected against long odds.

In my early days at the NCC, of course, I didn't much ponder such grand philosophical notions. I just worried about keeping my job. My official title was "Communications Director" which meant I wrote news releases, handled the group's media relations and stuffed lots of envelopes. The stuffing envelopes part I did pretty well, the other responsibilities, however, posed a bit more of a challenge. I quickly discovered, for instance, that my academic writing style didn't cut it when it came to media releases. Every time I would write a draft release and present it to David for his approval, he would rip it to shreds and bark at me, "This is boring! Punch it up." I had an even harder time when it came to drumming up media interest in NCC activities. A shy person by nature, I found it extremely stressful to call up journalists and producers with the aim of convincing them to cover NCC events or campaigns. Pitching stories to the media requires the skills and confidence of a salesman. And in my early days at the NCC, I made a lousy salesman. Plus David always had the idea that whatever he thought was interesting would also fascinate everybody else in the world. And that wasn't always true, which made my job difficult at times. Here's a how a typical media call might go:

"Hi, my name is Gerry Nicholls, I'm with the National Citizens Coalition, we ... the National Citizens Coalition ... it's a conservative group ... yes, we are the guys with the all the newspaper ads ... anyway, we are running an exciting ad campaign on the need to privatize sidewalks, maybe you would like to put our president David Somerville on your show so he can talk about it ... (click) hello ... hello ..."

More terrifying for me than pitching stories to the media was setting up news conferences. They were always hit and miss affairs. Sometimes we would hold a conference to a packed room of reporters. Other times nobody would show up. And when nobody showed up, David usually assumed I had not made the conference invitation interesting enough or that I hadn't called enough people. So on mornings of scheduled NCC news conferences, I was always on pins and needles. Would I be a hero or a scapegoat?

Despite my failings, however, David kept his confidence

in me. And I worked hard to get better. I took PR courses at night, read books on how to improve my writing skills and sought out the advice of others in my field. Gradually I got better and grew into the job, until, all modesty aside, I got dang good at it.

As I got better at doing what I did, the NCC got better at doing what it did.

CHAPTER 3
THE GOLDEN AGE

WHEN I STARTED WORKING AT THE NCC IN 1985 the organization was hardly high on anybody's credibility list. To be blunt, Canada's political and media establishment viewed us as nothing more than a collection of right-wing rabble-rousers operating on the far fringes of civilized debate. That's if they knew about us at all. Flash forward to 1997, however, and things were very different. We were still viewed as right-wing rabble-rousers, but as right-wing rabble-rousers who had the political clout to make a difference in this country. The media and politicians may not have liked us, but they had come to perceive us as a powerful political force, a force that had to be reckoned with and that could not be ignored. How did this transformation come to be? Well it's partly because the NCC's pro-free market agenda had by the late 1990s become more acceptable as far as mainstream thought was concerned. After all, even the Liberals were balancing the budget by that time. But mostly it was due to a series of groundbreaking campaigns the NCC waged in the 1980s and 1990s, both in the court of law and in the court of public opinion. It was these campaigns, as well as our ability to market them, which ultimately made the NCC an influential player on Canada's political stage.

Of course, these campaigns were not only important for the NCC, they were important for Canada, because they helped to promote and protect our economic and political freedoms. To go through them all would require a book on its own. So to save ink and paper, I will provide just a brief rundown of some of our more significant campaigns from the era I like to call the NCC's Golden Age.

NCC vs. Union Bosses

Like any conservative organization worth its salt, the NCC was primarily concerned with promoting the idea of individual freedom. And that included freedom for unionized employees. Simply put, we didn't think anybody should be forced to join, or pay dues to, a union. That didn't mean the NCC was anti-union, it just meant we believed in injecting a little democracy into the workplace. We believed unionized employees should have a choice. And it seemed to us back in the mid-1980s that the Charter of Rights and Freedoms should guarantee workers such a choice. After all, section 2D of the Charter stated quite clearly that all Canadians are guaranteed "freedom of association." Shouldn't that also mean the freedom *not* to associate? More specifically, shouldn't that mean no Canadian should be forced to associate with a union? We thought the answer to that question was yes. And so we decided to put our theory to the test.

In 1985 we hooked up with a community college teacher from Haileybury, Ontario named Merv Lavigne. Merv, while not a member of the Ontario Public Service Union (OPSEU), was forced, thanks to something called the Rand Formula, to pay union dues. And he objected to the fact that a portion of his forced dues were being used to finance political causes he didn't support, causes like the nuclear disarmament movement, the militant National Union of Mine Workers in the United Kingdom and the New Democratic Party. (Merv was a Liberal.) Merv's view was simple: when union bosses used his forced dues for political purposes they infringed on his right to free expression and on his right to free association. And Merv not only objected to this practice, he was determined to fight it. He wanted to take his union bosses to court to stop them from infringing on his freedom. After learning about Merv's courageous determination to fight for his rights, the NCC agreed to pay his legal bills.

For us, Merv's challenge wasn't just about helping one individual. It was about restoring freedom to all unionized employees who were forced to subsidize causes they didn't believe in.

Now let me be clear about one point: neither the NCC nor Merv Lavigne ever argued that unions had no business in politics. Rather, our view was that union bosses should only finance political causes with money unionized employees voluntarily donated for that purpose. Nor were we arguing that Merv shouldn't be forced to pay union dues. We were arguing that the dues he did pay be used for collective bargaining purposes and not to finance trendy left-wing causes. Sounds reasonable, right?

Well not to Canada's union bosses. In fact, Merv's challenge terrified them. Before long the National Union of Provincial Government Employees, the Canadian Labour Congress, the Ontario Federation of Labour and the Confederation of National Trade Unions all intervened in the case to oppose Merv's challenge. Merv and the NCC were taking on practically the entire organized labour movement in Canada.

Why did Merv scare union bosses so much? Why were they determined to see his challenge fail? Most likely it was because they realized that, if given a free choice, most rank and file union members wouldn't want to support their leftist causes. In fact, polls we commissioned at the time showed the vast majority of unionized employees supported Merv's stance. What the union bosses feared was that if Merv were successful, they would lose their ability to finance their political propaganda machine.

The first round in this epic clash went to Merv and the NCC. In June 1986, the Ontario Supreme Court ruled in Merv's favour. In his ruling, Justice John White wrote, "Compulsory dues may only be used for the purpose which justifies their imposition. In other words, the use of compulsory dues for purposes other than collective bargaining and collective agreement administration cannot be justified in a free and democratic society where the individual objects to such use." That ruling sent shockwaves through the union movement.

Unfortunately, in 1989 the Ontario Court of Appeal overturned Justice White's decision. That led to a dramatic legal showdown in the Supreme Court of Canada. I remember not feeling all that optimistic about our chances and it turned out my pessimism was justified. In 1991 the Supreme Court, in a 7-0 ruling no less, dismissed Merv's challenge. It was a fairly complicated ruling but essentially the Supreme Court justices decided that forcing employees to finance political beliefs against their will was not an infringement on freedom of association and even if it were, it was an infringement that could be justified in a free and democratic society. After all, reasoned the judges, unions do so much good in terms of promoting social causes. Barf.

Although our loss was a major disappointment, the Merv Lavigne court challenge was still a watershed moment in the NCC's history. We had played an important role in bringing forward a historic court challenge, meaning the NCC could no longer be dismissed as cranks. We were pushing the political envelope in this country. Not only did the Merv challenge mean more media attention for the NCC, it won us droves of new supporters. More supporters meant more donations, which in turn meant we could actually hire more staff, buy new office furniture and even purchase a few of those new-fangled computers.

The NCC vs. MP Pensions

One of the NCC's jobs was to expose and oppose government waste. And there was certainly plenty of it to expose and oppose. But one area of government waste that became our specialty was the Member of Parliament pension plan, which was far more lavish than anything anybody in the private sector could ever hope to afford. It's not for nothing that we called it the gold-plated MP pension plan.

First of all, MPs qualified for a pension after only six years of service. Second, it was fully indexed to inflation. Third, qualifying MPs could start collecting their pensions the day they left office, regardless of their age at the time. Finally, retired MPs could "double-dip." That is to say, they could collect their pensions even if they got another government job. We calculated that under this plan MPs could collect pensions worth up to a whopping $4 million. For us, this was red meat. It symbolized everything that was wrong with the governing political class – arrogance, extravagance, greed. So in 1990 we decided to make this pension plan an issue.

Our first strike occurred on September 4th, 1990. That's the day when an army of MPs, first elected in 1984, were going to qualify for their fat pension, as they had held office for six years. It was the perfect opportunity for a media hit. So we officially declared September 4th, 1990 to be Trough Day. In a news release announcing Trough Day, I described the qualifying MPs as greedy pigs jumping en masse into the pension trough. When Trough Day rolled around David Somerville held a news conference in Ottawa, just blocks away from the Parliament buildings. He was standing in front of a billboard which featured a cute cartoon pig lounging in a trough of dollars bills while sipping a glass of champagne. It was a great visual. The media loved it. We garnered tons of publicity on both TV and radio. I did about fifteen radio interviews in one day alone.

But that was just the beginning of our pension battle. For years after that we kept the pressure on with a series of anti-pension media campaigns. These campaigns were not only effective, they were fun. We had TV ads featuring real live pigs jostling in the mud. We had radio commercials with pigs oinking to the tune of the Blue Danube. And during the 1997 federal election campaign we launched what I called Operation Pork Chop. The latter was an ad campaign targeting 23 MPs – who if re-elected would have qualified for Parliamentary pensions – for defeat.

The campaign featured radio spots with squealing pigs and newspaper ads urging voters to "chop the pork." Of those we targeted, nine ended up losing their seats, the most prominent being Edmonton Liberal MP Judy Bethel. We also very nearly knocked off Anne McLellan, a Liberal cabinet minister.

When the election was over, we generated more publicity for the cause by releasing our estimates as to how much defeated MPs who had qualified for their pensions would rake in. In a news release David Somerville announced, "Of all the MPs who met defeat … eight had qualified for the lavish MP pension. That means that although they lost the election they won the MP pension lottery."

Eventually our pressure produced results.

The Reform Party, for instance, adopted the NCC's anti-MP pension stance and in 1995 virtually every Reform MP, in an act of admirable principle, opted out of the plan. To mark that event David Somerville held a news conference in Ottawa – during which he handed Reform MP Deborah Grey a bouquet of roses – to congratulate the Reform caucus. (Unfortunately, in 2001 many of those MPs, including Grey, jumped back into the pension trough.) Even the Liberals got the message, which led them to reform the MP pension plan, at least a bit. The government ended the double-dipping and instituted an age limit so that MPs could not start collecting pensions until age 55.

I should also mention that while our MP pension campaign was popular with the general public and with the media, we did get one complaint. It was from the Canadian Swine Breeders' Association. They said our ad campaign was unfair to pigs.

The NCC also had a couple of noteworthy political battles with our ideological opposites – the socialist New Democratic Party. One battle was waged against former NDP leader Ed Broadbent, the other against Bob Rae, during his ill-fated reign as Ontario's Premier.

The Broadbent campaign was a short but intense mêlée that occurred before and during the 1988 federal election. In the summer of that year Arthur Finkelstein had done a poll for us on Canadian attitudes towards political parties. What he discovered shocked us. According to Arthur's poll, a whopping 40 percent of Canadians supported the NDP, meaning the socialists could actually form the next government. Arthur told us his findings indicated Canadians liked Broadbent because they viewed him as more honest than either Prime Minister Brian Mulroney or Liberal leader John Turner. Ed Broadbent as Prime Minister of Canada? The horror! The horror! (Reference to *Heart of Darkness*)Something had to be done. Somebody had to undermine public support for Broadbent and the NDP. We took on the task.

Luckily, Arthur's poll also revealed Broadbent's Achilles heel: the more Canadians learned about his agenda, the less likely they were to support him. In other words, they liked Broadbent, but not his socialist ideas. So we put together an ad campaign to link the popular NDP leader to his party's unpopular left-wing agenda. Our theme was that Ed Broadbent was "very, very scary."

We launched our campaign in mid-August 1988 because we knew a federal election would be called in the fall and we wanted to get our hits in as early as possible. It was the largest media blitz in our history. We spent $500,000 on radio spots, newspaper ads and direct mail.

One of our radio ads featured two guys – Harry and George – having a conversation. The ad copy went something like this:

George: Hey Harry, I see you are wearing an Ed Broadbent button.

Harry: Yeah, he's my kind of guy.

George: Did you know he wants to take Canada out of NATO. It's kept the peace for over 40 years and he wants to pull out.

Harry: I didn't know that. That's scary.

George: And did you know that Broadbent is against Senate reform.

Harry: No I didn't know that either. That's scary.

George: So why are you wearing that Ed Broadbent button?

Harry: Good question.

Announcer: NDP leader Ed Broadbent is very, very scary.

Another radio ad was supposed to sound like a game show:

Host: Welcome to the Very, Very Scary Game. First question, which leader wants to pull Canada out of NATO?

Contestant 1: Karl Marx.

Contestant 2: Groucho Marx.

Contestant 3: Ed Broadbent.

Host: Yes that's right. Ed Broadbent wants to pull Canada out of NATO. He's very, very scary.

We got a lot of flak from the media over this campaign. People said we were unfairly smearing a popular politician.

But from a PR perspective the campaign was a major hit. It generated lots of coverage precisely because it was controversial and hard-hitting. It also worked in terms of driving down NDP support, especially in British Columbia, where much of our ad campaign was focused. Polls indicated NDP support in the province was dropping. Yes, our Very, Very Scary campaign was a big success by any measure. But there was one tiny problem. About two weeks after the election was called our campaign became completely irrelevant.

What happened was that almost overnight the 1988 election went from being a contest between political parties, to a referendum on freer trade with the United States. The Progressive Conservatives supported freer trade while the Liberals opposed the pact and in the process became the champions of economic nationalism. This left Broadbent and his very, very scary agenda on the sidelines, a non-issue as far as the election was concerned. This meant we had to change gears overnight. We had to go from bashing the NDP to promoting freer trade. And that's what we did. We spent about $200,000 on pro-free trade TV and newspaper ads.

Part of the problem with pushing free trade, however, was that a lot of Canadians (and for that matter a lot of NCC supporters) just didn't like Prime Minister Brian Mulroney. In other words, we had to sell the idea of free trade, despite Mulroney. Or as Arthur so indelicately put it during one of our strategy sessions, "We have to convince Canadians to drink pig piss."

So we figured if we couldn't drive up support for the Tories maybe we could do the next best thing and help drive down support for the Liberals. To do that, we ran a newspaper ad Machiavellian in its cleverness. To the unwary observer the ad was a typical right-wing assault on the NDP. The headline was, "Look Who's Opposing Free Trade." And under a photo of Broadbent the ad copy declared, "Ed Broadbent: A dedicated socialist, who means what he says. He doesn't believe in free enterprise. He doesn't believe in free trade. He's very, very scary."

But the ad also had a subliminal message directed at NDPers who were thinking of strategically voting Liberal to stop free trade. That message was, "Hey, we nasty right-wingers at the NCC are attacking your guy because he's a true socialist. Are you going to let us get away with that?"

Get it? We were sneakily using psychology to drive NDPers back home. After all, it's a natural emotional reaction for people to rally around their friends when they are under attack. We wanted left-wingers to rally around Broadbent.

The ad appeared in the *Globe and Mail* on the Friday before the election and it certainly got a reaction. I was working in the office the next day and fielded about two dozen or so calls from outraged leftists. Our scheme was working. And of course, the Tories went on to win that election and freer trade became a reality.

Our battle against NDP Ontario Premier Bob Rae lasted longer – about four years. Rae, to a lot of people's horror, won a majority government in the fall of 1990. This meant that Ontario, the economic engine of Canada, was in the hands of the Red Menace. Talk about very, very scary.

And our worst fears about the NDP were confirmed in the spring of 1991 when Rae's first budget boosted both taxes and government spending. That's when he declared he was proud to be fighting the recession rather than the deficit. This guy was a disaster; we had to stop him.

One problem we faced in battling Rae, however, was that the NCC was a national organization. We couldn't expect NCC supporters in Alberta or British Columbia to subsidize a campaign centered solely in Ontario. So we decided to create a project group called Ontarians for Responsible Government (ORG). This group had its own letterhead, its own separate newsletter and its own fundraising appeals, but it was still run by the NCC. It had one purpose and one purpose only: to wage an all-out electoral war against Bob Rae. We wanted to wipe the NDP off the map.

And so from 1991 until 1995, ORG ran a series of TV, newspaper and radio ads to expose what we called "Bob Rae's ruinous economic agenda." Interestingly, our most potent media weapon in opposing Rae turned out to be billboard ads. In 1991 we rented a billboard in downtown Toronto, just blocks from the Ontario legislature. And every month or so we would put up a new anti-Rae billboard message, messages I endeavoured to make witty, graphically interesting and just a tad controversial.

My favorite billboard was the one which featured a photo of a mousetrap labelled "mouse killer," a photo of a fly swatter labelled "Bug Killer," and a photo of Bob Rae labelled, "Job Killer." Another billboard lambasted the premier's attempt to unionize farm workers by featuring the premier's photo next to the picture of a donkey, with a caption reading, "Which One Wants to Unionize the Family Farm?"

Fairly inexpensive to rent, these billboards attracted a tremendous amount of media attention. Reporters loved them and actually looked forward to what our billboards would say next. Over time our Toronto billboard even became something of a political landmark, and people in the Ontario legislative press gallery started referring to us as "the billboard people."

Not that billboard advocacy didn't have risks. One time our chairman drove to Peterborough to show off a new anti-Rae billboard to the local media. But things didn't go according to plan. He called me up in a state of agitation. "Gerry, what the hell is going on? I am standing here with reporters and photographers in front of a damn Kentucky Fried Chicken ad!!" Turns out due to a miscommunication our billboard didn't go up on time. That was a little embarrassing for the Chairman and very discomforting for me.

Nevertheless despite such setbacks our billboards did have a political impact. Just ask Bob Rae or better yet, read his memoirs. Obviously still stinging from the billboard attacks, Rae lashed out at us, writing, "The National Citizens Coalition, a shadowy front group with big money, had already rented a billboard just around the corner from Queen's Park, displaying posters worthy of Allende's Chile."[6]

Why were these billboards so successful? Simple. They offered concise but hard-hitting messages which conveyed the frustrations of Ontarians fed up with big government and high taxes. More importantly they provided a perfect photo-op for the media to illustrate those frustrations.

Anyway, our anti-Rae campaign went into overdrive during the provincial election of 1995. The NCC spent close to half a million dollars in a campaign that threw everything we had at the Premier: TV spots, newspaper ads, radio commercials. And during the last week of the election, when polls indicated Rae was heading for a massive defeat, we put up one last anti-Rae billboard. It featured a photo of the premier waving his hand next to the caption, "So Long Bob, Socialism Didn't Work." Photos of that billboard appeared in papers across the country and actually popped up in American publications. It perfectly encapsulated the failure that was Rae.

I am much too modest to suggest that my ORG campaign played a key role in ensuring Bob Rae's defeat. So I will quote a news release from the federal Liberal Party of Canada which declared, "The NCC has mobilized expensive and aggressive campaigns aimed at affecting the outcome of elections; for example, it founded Ontarians for Responsible Government: a lobby group which played a large role in electing the Harris government in Ontario."[7]

I rest my case.

The NCC's most important campaign had nothing to do with pigs or pensions or politicians. It involved something a little more important to democracy: the right to free political speech. The NCC was forced to defend this crucial freedom time and time again because politicians kept trying to muzzle us by enacting election gag laws. These laws essentially imposed strict legal restrictions on how much money citizens or independent groups – like the NCC – could spend during elections on political advertising.

The first such gag law surfaced in late 1983. Then Prime Minister Pierre Trudeau amended Canada's Elections Act to ensure third parties would no longer have a say in the democratic process. His amendments, officially called Bill C-169, made it illegal for non-politicians to spend any money during federal elections to support or oppose a political party or candidate. Bill C-169 made it illegal for the NCC to produce a bumper sticker saying, "Don't Vote Liberal," or to pass out buttons that read, "Stop Trudeau's Left-wing Agenda," or to run newspaper ads criticizing the government's economic policies. This law wouldn't just silence the NCC. It would have silenced all independent voices – business organizations, labour unions, church groups, all would have been gagged. To be blunt, Trudeau was making free political speech a crime. Bill C-169 was all about giving political parties a monopoly on election debate and forcing everybody else to shut up. Trudeau's gag law was not only undemocratic, it was anti-democratic.

Now you would think such a radical measure to stifle free expression would have sparked some opposition in Parliament. It didn't. All three parties at the time – the NDP, the Liberals and even the Progressive Conservatives – eagerly supported Trudeau's gag law. Incredibly, it was passed by the House of Commons after only 45 minutes of debate! And so, in less time than it takes to have lunch, Canada's political parties scrapped a right crucial to any free society.

In fact, this law would have infringed on the democratic rights of all Canadians, not just those who wished to run political ads. Free speech is a two way street; it means not only having the freedom to speak out, but also having the freedom to hear different ideas and viewpoints. Trudeau's gag law made that impossible.

Only one group in Canada opposed this law from the beginning – the National Citizens Coalition. In early 1984 the NCC used a full-page newspaper ad to announce it was launching a constitutional challenge to the gag law. The ad explained what was at stake and asked for financial help to pay for the legal costs of the challenge. "I refuse to be muzzled. I'm fighting back," declared a coupon attached to the ad. The response to the NCC request was overwhelming – the ad campaign raised more than $300,000.

Soon, many in the media joined the NCC in attacking the gag law. A *Toronto Sun* editorial declared the law's passage "may be the lowest point in the history of free speech and democracy in this country." The *Edmonton Journal* said, "There is now an official monopoly on who may participate in federal elections." A *Globe and Mail* editorial noted MPs "have now ensured that total control of printed and published material during election campaigns will rest with politicians." The Canadian Daily Newspaper Association also denounced Trudeau's gag law.

On the other side of the debate, the Liberals argued the gag law was needed to stop the "rich from buying elections." Unfortunately for them, however, they had no evidence elections could be bought. None. That's why, in June 1984, Justice Don Medhurst of the Alberta Court of Queen's Bench struck down Trudeau's gag law as unconstitutional, saying it violated section 2b of the Charter of Rights and Freedoms which guarantees the right to free expression. The gag law was officially dead. The NCC had restored a basic democratic freedom to all Canadians. But like some monster in a cheap science fiction movie, the gag law would not stay dead.

In April 1993, it was resurrected when then Prime Minister Brian Mulroney enacted his own gag law, a gag law very similar to Trudeau's, except this time groups and individuals would be allowed to spend up to $1,000 on political advertising. Once again, politicians were seeking to deny citizens the right to spend their own money to express their own views during elections. What made this a little ironic was that during the 1984 election Mulroney had apologized for his party's support of Trudeau's gag law, saying he had been "asleep at the switch." So why the change? Why was Mulroney now pro-gag law?

Well, it all stemmed back to the 1988 federal election. Thanks to the NCC's court victory in 1984, that election was gag law free, which meant groups and citizens could spend as much as they wanted to promote their ideas and viewpoints. And spend they did. Groups like the Canadian Alliance for Trade and Job Opportunities spent about $3.6 million on pro-free trade advertising. Anti-free trade groups meanwhile spent about $878,000[8]. To us at the NCC, this was good news. The more people who got involved in the political process the better, the more debate there was about issues the better. As David Somerville put it, the 1988 election was "an outstanding example of how we would like to see democracy function."

To others, however – most notably left-wingers sour at losing the free trade debate – the 1988 federal election was unfair because one side spent more than the other. This was the "we can't allow the rich to buy votes" argument. It's an argument based on the premise that Canadian voters are easily misled simpletons who can be bamboozled by glitzy advertising campaigns. It was always our view at the NCC that Canadian voters are actually pretty bright. They make their decisions based on the facts and issues, not on how much money one side spends. In other words, Canadian voters supported freer trade not because one side spent more money than the other, but simply because freer trade happened to be a good idea.

Nevertheless, the Mulroney government decided to set up a Royal Commission on Electoral Reform and Party Financing (better known as the Lortie Commission) to study the question. In 1992 the Lortie Commission, worried about the effects of unregulated spending, recommended the government impose a new gag law and the government complied.

So once again, in the name of protecting free speech, the NCC went to court to fight the gag law. And once again the courts ruled in our favour. In 1993 Justice Macleod of the Alberta Court of Queen's Bench found that since the government provided no evidence proving unregulated political spending harmed democracy, gag laws could not be justified in a free and democratic society. The government, now under Prime Minister Kim Campbell, appealed that ruling. In 1996 the government lost again. The Alberta Court of Appeal also ruled the gag law to be unconstitutional. In her ruling, Justice Carole Conrad stated election gag laws imposed a dangerous limit on free expression and that their real purpose was to give a "privileged voice to political parties and official candidates within those parties." Again, the NCC had restored a basic democratic freedom to all Canadians. The government didn't appeal that ruling, meaning the Mulroney gag law, like the Trudeau gag law, was dead.

We were overjoyed with our victory, but our joy was tempered by the knowledge that this fight probably wasn't over. As David Somerville told the media, "We expect they will now go back to the drawing board and try and dream up a new gag law for the next election." And indeed, in 2000, the government did go back to the gag law drawing board. But that's a story for later in this book.

You might get the idea from all of this that, during the NCC's Golden Age, politicians and political parties were our main enemies. And you would be right. But it didn't have to be that way. In fact, our goal was for political parties to adapt and copy our ideas. And that did happen in one case. When the Reform Party emerged in the late 1980s, its initial policy platform – with its support for direct democracy, balanced budgets and lower taxes – bore a striking resemblance to the NCC's agenda. As David Somerville put it, "the Reform Party has cribbed probably two-thirds of our policy book." That didn't happen by coincidence. David, who attended the party's founding convention in 1987, later estimated that nearly half of the attending delegates were NCC supporters. It was just another example of how the NCC influenced Canada's political agenda.

By the late 1990s, the NCC was truly making a difference.

I was proud to be a part of it.

CHAPTER 4
JUST CALL ME CHE GUEVARA

THE SUCCESS OF THE NCC COMPLETELY FLUMMOXED Canada's left-wingers. They couldn't quite figure out how a supposedly "virulently right-wing and anti-government organization"[9] like the NCC could not only exist in Canada, but thrive.

After all, wasn't Canada supposed to a "progressive" socialist bastion? Maybe groups like the NCC could flourish in the United States, but not here. The only plausible explanation had to be that the NCC was not a real organization at all, but some sort of front group with secret sources of funding. A front group for whom?

Take your pick. At one time or another we were labelled a front group for the Conservative Party, the Reform Party, the Liberal Party, the American government, the Israeli government, oil companies, the military-industrial complex and the CIA. Most often, however, we were simply called a front for "big business." As former union boss Dennis McDermott once put it, the NCC is a "front for some of the wealthiest and most powerful corporations and individuals in the country."[10] No doubt, McDermott pictured NCC officials getting together in a dimly lit room with a small group of cigar-smoking, top hat-wearing capitalists who would hand us huge sacks of cash so we could put up more pig billboards.

I kind of wish it had been like that. It sure would have made the fundraising a lot easier. The reality, however, was that the NCC had few Bay Street supporters. Corporate Canada, for the most part, stayed away from us because we were deemed too controversial and we rocked too many boats. That's not to say we didn't have wealthy contributors who could cut us big cheques from time to time (God bless them). But for the most part the NCC relied on the support of people who contributed $50 or $75 or $100. In other words, the NCC was what we always claimed it was: a grassroots organization. And raising money in a grassroots fashion isn't easy. Unlike political parties, we did not have charitable status, meaning contributors received no tax credit for supporting us. Unlike many left-wing groups, the NCC did not receive or ask for government handouts. Unlike union bosses, we could not coerce individuals to finance our campaigns. Instead, the NCC relied 100 percent on voluntary contributions from people who believed in what we were doing. Go figure! That's why every NCC ad, every newsletter, every communication, every NCC event, always included a request for financial aid. And we mailed a lot of fundraising letters to both supporters and potential supporters.

At our peak, we took in about $2.8 million a year in revenue. That's a lot of money but hardly the unlimited corporate cash of the Left's fervid imagination. In fact, our opponents – political parties, union bosses, governments – could always outspend us. If anything, from a resources point of view, the NCC was a David fighting an army of Goliaths.

So, if it wasn't secret supplies of corporate cash which accounted for the NCC's success, what did? Well, for one thing, we were good at getting the biggest bang for our buck. What we lacked in money and resources we made up for with moxie and clever marketing. Or to put it another way, the NCC excelled at what I like to call political guerilla warfare.

Like a guerilla army, the NCC was careful to avoid pitched battles against superior forces. We attacked only vulnerable targets. Then we escaped into the mountains until the time was right to strike again.

The NCC's Merv Lavigne campaign was a good example of guerrilla warfare. We didn't take on the broad question of whether or not employees should be forced to join a union. Rather, we zeroed in on the weakest, least defensible aspect of forced unionism – compelling employees, through their forced union dues, to support a political cause against their will. It doesn't take a lot of persuading to convince Canadians that this is an unfair, undemocratic practice that must be stopped.

Likewise, it's easy to mobilize public opinion against government waste if you link it to something unpopular ... like politicians. That's what we did with our campaign against gold-plated MP pensions. Politicians are always vulnerable targets because nobody wants to defend them. Nobody has sympathy for them.

The other good thing about politicians is I could always count on them to do a little spinning for me. Spinning is what we called it when a politician would react to an NCC attack by lashing out against us publicly. I loved it when that happened. After all, the NCC attacking a politician was not necessarily news, but a politician attacking us usually guaranteed us some headlines. And that's simply because the media like drama and conflict. The NCC getting embroiled in a public brawl with some high profile political personality was good copy.

Plus, whenever a politician attacked us it gave the NCC credibility. It was proof we mattered, that we were having an impact. As a result, it was also good for fundraising. If left-wing politicians were attacking the NCC it meant we were doing something right and consequently our supporters would rally to our side.

That's why if MPs had been smart, they would have ignored us when we went after them. Luckily for me, politicians usually weren't smart. Maybe it's their egos but they just don't like to be criticized. Sheila Copps, for instance, would always spin for us. Whenever we singled her out in one of our campaigns, she would inevitably take the bait and screechingly denounce the NCC at the top of her lungs. It was music to my ears. And sometimes to ensure retaliation we would purposely taunt our political opponents. When we launched a campaign to defeat Tory MP Jim Hawkes, for example, we held a news conference right outside of his Calgary campaign headquarters. We were daring him to take a shot at us, which he did.

Of course, to be effective, political guerrilla warfare campaigns also require creative communication strategies. And creative campaigns are simple campaigns: the simpler your message the better. That's why we stayed away from complexity and substance, choosing instead to frame our message in a concise, straightforward manner. We were not a think tank. We didn't release reports or studies or complicated analyses.

Instead, what we aimed to do was focus on people's emotions, to push hot-button issues. Rather than getting people to think, our campaigns were designed to get people to react. We wanted them to get angry: angry at bad government, angry at union boss bullying, angry at high taxes and angry at arrogant, wasteful politicians. In politics anger is good. Angry people are easier to mobilize. Angry voters are more likely to give you a donation and more likely to take political action.

We were also good at defining issues to our advantage. I call this winning the war of the words. For instance, the NCC definitely won the war of the words when it came to fighting election gag laws precisely because we defined them as "gag laws," a term which sounds sinister and undemocratic. And the media picked up on it. Journalists starting calling limits on free election speech "gag laws," and not just in editorials but in straight news stories. Consequently, anybody reading those stories would likely sympathize with the NCC because who wants to support laws that gag people? We did the same thing when we labelled the MP pension plan "gold-plated." The media and the public adopted this phraseology, helping us spin the story in our favour.

The NCC was also skillful in using the media to get our message out. Yes, I know many conservatives see the media as left-wing and biased, which they are. But biased or not, getting media coverage for a campaign is crucial if you don't have lots of money. Media coverage, after all, is basically free advertising. In fact, sometimes it's even better than free advertising, because you can't buy an ad on the front page of a newspaper.

That's why our ad campaigns were crafted in order to attract media attention. They were controversial or innovative or eye-catching. (Think pigs on billboards.) And it paid off. Take our anti-Bob Rae billboard campaign. Those relatively inexpensive billboards garnered the NCC tens of thousands of dollars of free publicity. It wasn't because all that many people saw them as they strolled by, but because images of the billboard appeared in newspaper stories and on national TV news shows.

In short, even left-wing journalists can't resist a good story, and that's what the NCC always strove to give them. As part of our media strategy, I made sure to cultivate good relationships with columnists, talk show hosts and journalists. I was always prepared for interviews. I worked hard to come up with interesting sound bites and quotes, and most importantly, I always told the truth.

Overall, I can't complain about the way the media treated the NCC. Yes, there were some journalists who had an axe to grind and who would print blatant lies about us. But for the most part, I found the media to be fair and balanced when covering the NCC. In a way, it was a value for value relationship. I provided the media with informed conservative commentary and with interesting campaigns to write about. They, in turn, gave the NCC exposure.

Not that all NCC campaigns were a rousing success. One campaign in particular, a campaign I like to call the Dawson Creek Massacre, was a major flop. It occurred back in the mid-1980s, a time when Canada was in a terrible fiscal mess – massive deficits, soaring national debt and out of control government spending. We decided to raise public awareness about the country's economic woes. We wanted to warn Canadians how the government's wasteful spending policies were threatening the future of the country. So we put together an ad campaign with lots of charts and graphs and economic statistics. We talked about the $40 billion deficits and the $500 billion national debt and about taxes and about how much money politicians were spending on massive boondoggles. We had newspaper ads and TV spots and radio commercials. It seemed like a slam dunk campaign.

To be on the safe side, though, we decided to test market our message in Dawson Creek, British Columbia. And it's a good thing we did. The campaign didn't catch on at all. Nobody reacted to it. Nobody cared. We were flabbergasted. Where, we wondered, did we go wrong? To find out, we did a little survey which told us something interesting. What we discovered was that nobody really understood what we were talking about. Our target audience didn't understand the terms of the debate. Words like deficit or debt didn't really mean anything to them. Nor could they relate to the astronomical budgetary numbers we were tossing around. Our message simply wasn't getting through.

We learned from that failure and came up with a better way to attack government waste. Rather than focusing on the big abstract picture, we went after the problem on a micro-level by exposing the outrageous ways politicians were squandering tax dollars. We researched and collected hundreds and hundreds of examples of ridiculous government misspending. We found out, for instance, that the federal government spent $15,000 to fund something called "The Continuous Garbage Project" and $20,000 for a two-act play entitled, "The Ecstasy of Bedridden Riding Hood" and $38,000 for a study on the Detroit Tigers and $21,000 for a study called "Deviancy and the new woman." (OK, that study on female deviancy might have some value.) Then we took our examples of appalling government waste and put them in a little booklet entitled,

"Tales from the Tax Trough." This booklet had no charts. No graphs. No statistics. What it did have was plenty of cartoon pigs, an easy-to-read writing style and this message to taxpayers: "The National Citizens Coalition believes governments should leave more of people's money in their own pockets, rather than letting it go to wasteful government spending initiatives."

We then mailed out thousands of these little booklets. We mailed them to our supporters, to businesses, to the media, to politicians, to anyone we thought might be interested. We also launched a multimedia ad campaign to market the booklets to the general public. And, unlike the Dawson Creek Massacre, this time we hit a home run. For one thing, the media loved the concept. TV news shows, newspapers, magazines – all of them – picked up on our booklet story. I had radio shows lining up around the block to interview me, so I could list off some of the examples of waste we had uncovered. It was great theatre.

The public loved our booklet too. In fact, so many people were asking us to mail them a copy of "Tales" we could barely keep up with the demand. We were literally shipping them out by the box loads.

Our little booklets also caught Ottawa's attention, but not in a good way. The Tories were not pleased. Then Finance Minister Michael Wilson even set up a meeting with David Somerville to talk about them. When David showed up at the Minister's office, Wilson tossed a copy of the "Tales" booklet on his desk and asked disdainfully, "What the hell is this?" Clearly, the government was feeling some heat.

Why was this campaign so successful? Because rather than discussing the theoretical impact of government spending we offered concrete examples of where tax dollars were going. Telling a taxpayer the government has a deficit of $40 billion might not get a reaction. But telling that same taxpayer that he is paying $105,000 on a study comparing hockey coaches and symphony conductors probably will.

Getting taxpayers to react is more than half the battle. Once you catch their attention, once you get them thinking about government waste, it's easier to make the case for smaller government and lower taxes. In fact, I bet our little cartoon pigs did more to educate Canadians about government waste than all of the think tanks and all of the economic studies combined. The "Tales" campaign, in short, was the perfect example of how a guerrilla political warfare operation should work.

But I don't want to get too wrapped up in talking about the NCC's marketing wizardry. Although it was an important factor in our success, it was not the most crucial factor. What was the most crucial factor? That's easy. The NCC had the most magnificently generous and loyal supporters in the world. Without their steadfast moral and financial support the NCC wouldn't and couldn't exist. It's that simple.

Time and time again, we asked our supporters to help to finance costly court challenges or media ad campaigns, and each and every time they responded heroically. I was always amazed and awed at how NCC supporters would rise to the occasion, no matter the odds, no matter the foe. They utterly refused to ever give up. These were people who not only believed in freedom but who were willing to fight for it. I was proud to be associated with such a remarkable group of Canadians.

Who were these NCC supporters? They came from all parts of the country and from all walks of life and represented the whole spectrum of conservative thought. Among our supporters were social conservatives, fiscal conservatives, neo-conservatives, libertarians, anti-gun control advocates, evangelical Christians and even a blue Liberal or two. The typical NCC supporter was a small businessman or a self-employed entrepreneur or simply a conservative activist. Many were senior citizens. And while they may have differed in many ways, all NCC supporters had one thing in common – a belief in the idea of more freedom through less government. What bound them together was ideology and the conviction that big government didn't have all the answers.

Incidentally, we kept the names of our supporter confidential and refused to release their names to the media or to anybody else. Left-wingers always like to make a big deal out of this. They seemed to think it proved the NCC was menacing and secretive. In the 2006 federal election, for instance, union boss Buzz Hargrove snidely referred to the NCC as a "secret society."[11] (What kind of secret society buys full-page newspaper ads and TV commercials?) What Buzz and other leftist critics didn't seem to understand was that there's a big difference between "secret" and "confidential." Nothing stopped NCC supporters from proclaiming their support for our organization. They were free to shout it from the rooftops! In fact, we encouraged our supporters to tell their friends, family and business associates about us. The best form of advertising we found was a personal recommendation. But we would not reveal the names of NCC supporters to the public or to the media without their permission.

Partly, we did this out of principle. Canadians have a right to keep their political views private. It's why we have the secret ballot. But mostly we did this to protect our supporters from possible retaliation. What sort of retaliation? Well, let's say you are running a business and are seeking a contract with the government. Some vindictive politician could possibly hold it against you were he to find out you belonged to a group that attacked his pension. Or worse, you might find yourself getting audited. And the government wasn't the only potential threat. Union bosses could also make life difficult for businesses that were known to support the NCC. And they could also make it hard for unionized employees who gave us their support. One time, in fact, a union official actually threatened to rip up the union card of any employee who was also an NCC member. No one should lose their job simply because of their political opinions.

And the NCC was successful for one other reason. We were non-partisan, independent of all political parties. What mattered to us were ideas, not political labels. If the

Liberals did something we liked, we praised them; if the Progressive Conservatives did something we didn't like, we attacked them, and vice versa.

It was this independence which gave the NCC credibility and which made us a legitimate voice for the Canadian conservative movement. We realized that the minute we were perceived as puppets for politicians would be the minute we would cease to be effective. That's why Colin set up the NCC head office in Toronto, not Ottawa. We wanted to keep politicians an arm's length away.

That's why it was a little ironic that in 1997, we took a politician into our midst. In fact, he became our president. His name was Stephen Harper.

CHAPTER 5
STEPHEN HARPER
TAKES THE REINS

IN 1995, DAVID SOMERVILLE ANNOUNCED THAT IN THREE years he would give up his job as NCC president so he could make some money in the real world. He wanted to give the organization as much time as possible to find and train a suitable replacement. The question was, who would replace him?

The NCC's Board of Directors instituted a search process shrouded in secrecy. None of us on staff knew even who was interviewing for the position. But in the fall of 1996, when Reform MP Stephen Harper announced he was not seeking re-election, I knew he would get the job.

"You watch," I predicted, ad nauseam, to my co-workers. "Stephen Harper will be our next president." Turns out I was right. On the morning of January 13th, 1997, David held a staff meeting to introduce us to our next boss – Stephen Harper. The next day David and Stephen held a news conference in Ottawa to make it official.

So how did I know Stephen would get the job? Was I clairvoyant? No. It was nothing more than simple, old-fashioned, logical deduction. The list of potential candidates – people who would have the proper skill set to run an organization like the NCC – was not that long. President of the National Citizens Coalition is not a run-of-the-mill job.

First of all, you need to be an ideologically pure, small "c" conservative. That means you must reject Pierre Trudeau and all of his works. You must view the CBC as a socialist-run boondoggle. In general, you must believe that whatever the private sector can do, the public sector can do – worse.

You must also know how to communicate effectively. You must know how to handle hostile media interviews and how to boil down complex socio-political issues into tidy 15 second sound bites. And you must have the debating skills to take on everyone from union bosses, to left-wing academics, to politicians and to NCC supporters who want a refund because the latest newsletter contained a split-infinitive.

And you must have no compunction about picking up the phone and asking a successful businessman for a $5,000 donation to help pay for radio ads featuring pigs oinking to the tune of the Blue Danube.

To me Stephen Harper fit the bill. Not only was he known as a principled ideological conservative, but as a Reform

MP he had been a consistent and forceful champion of NCC causes. He spoke out vehemently against the MP pension plan, he denounced the Mulroney government's election gag law and he ensured that NCC representatives could appear before House of Commons' committees. What's more, Stephen was a long-time member of the NCC and had spoken at some of our events. Plus, I knew David liked Stephen. The two had first met back in 1987 at one of the Reform Party's founding conventions and had become friends. Many times David would tell me how impressed he was with this "bright, young Calgary MP."

This is not to suggest, however, that the NCC and Stephen Harper had any sort of official relationship before he became our president. Some have claimed, for instance, that the NCC ran an ad campaign in the 1993 election specifically aimed at defeating Tory MP Jim Hawkes so that Stephen could win a seat in the House of Commons. This story has been making the rounds for years and it even resurfaced during the 2008 federal election.[12] Total nonsense!

True, during the 1993 federal election the NCC did run a $50,000 ad campaign to defeat Jim Hawkes, the popular PC incumbent in the riding of Calgary-West. And it's also true that Stephen Harper was his main rival. But our battle against Hawkes had nothing to do with Harper; it was actually part of the NCC's war against election gag laws.

Unfortunately for Hawkes, he was the government's point

man and chief public defender of Mulroney's gag law. That made him a marked man. He had to be defeated. And by defeated, I don't mean we wanted him to lose. I mean we wanted to crush Hawkes, to grind him into little bits of Tory dust. We wanted to send an unmistakable message to politicians: if you support gag laws, get ready to pay a steep price. As Arthur Finkelstein put it, we wanted to serve "Hawkes' head on a platter."

That's why we hammered Hawkes with everything in our arsenal. We used newspaper ads, radio spots and TV commercials – all of which linked Hawkes to the gag law. And it worked. Hawkes went down to flaming defeat. To us this campaign was not about Harper winning, but about Hawkes losing. In fact, Stephen's name was never mentioned at any of the many strategy meetings we held to discuss the Hawkes campaign.

But back to our story.

When the media learned about Harper's jump to the NCC they were a little stunned. Why would a politician widely considered a rising star quit partisan politics? Did he plan to challenge for the Reform Party leadership one day? Was the NCC simply to be Stephen's Elba, a place of exile where he could plot his triumphant return to politics?

The answer Stephen gave the media was, "No." He patiently repeated again and again that he joined the NCC to free himself from the shackles of partisan politics. He believed he could do more for Canada and for the conservative movement by leading the NCC than he could by being an opposition MP. Here's how Stephen himself put it in the NCC newsletter:

The truth is that, in the past decade, the political arena has begun to fill with politicians and political organizations struggling to implement the basic values for which the NCC has always stood, at one time very much alone. The agenda of the NCC was a guide to me as the founding policy director of Reform.

I have long supported and proudly defended the NCC and it has never given me reason to do otherwise.

Elected officials are constrained by the need for popularity every four to five years. The average one is consumed by the monthly opinion polls. The really bad ones worry about the approval of every group coming through their offices looking for a handout. Working with you in the NCC provides me with an opportunity to do much more – to fight for basic conservative values of free markets and free elections, whether fashionable at that moment or not.

I am honoured to join you in your fight. The battle for political and economic freedom will have its victories and setbacks, as it has in the past.

It will never end … and we shall never surrender.

Mind you, Stephen did not assume leadership of the NCC right off the bat. For the first year, he was the NCC's vice president working alongside David in our Calgary office, which had opened up in 1994. David figured it would take Stephen a year to learn the ropes before he would be ready to assume the presidency. So for most of 1997 he and Stephen shared a cramped little office in downtown Calgary.

It was an arrangement, unfortunately, that ultimately helped to destroy their friendship. The NCC was just not a big enough environment in which two type-A personalities could peacefully co-exist. It rankled Stephen no end to take orders from David, especially when those orders were sometimes demeaning. "Do you know what Somerville has me doing?" he once complained to me. "He has me clipping articles out of the bloody newspaper." Nevertheless, Stephen hung in there, biding his time and clipping newspapers.

On December 12th, 1997, his wait was over. That day marked our last staff meeting with David as our president. It was a sad moment. I had worked with David for nearly ten years and had come to admire his passion for the cause. Sure, he could be strident at times, but he gave the NCC and the cause of freedom everything he had to give. In fact, I think the reason he decided to quit was that he was just burned out. But during his presidency the NCC had made great strides. David increased our support base and modernized the operation. He made the NCC more of a substantial corporation.

Before he left, David took one last moment to gaze upon the old NCC framed newspaper ads which adorned the office walls. Then, his eyes welling up with tears, he walked out the door. David was gone. An era was over. Stephen Harper was now our president and our future.

We on the staff were excited by the prospect of Stephen taking up the reins. We had the sense he was a star who could take the NCC to dazzling new heights.

But star or not, we also had to adjust quickly to life under the Harper regime. His style of leadership, as it turned out, was quite different than what we were used to under David.

For one thing, David was an impulsive, almost rash "damn the torpedoes, full steam ahead" sort of decision maker. If he saw something on the morning news that upset him, he wanted an NCC campaign ready to go that afternoon. Where David loved the combat of politics, Stephen liked the planning, plotting and strategizing. He was methodical and cautious. Before he undertook any campaign he liked to think it through, plan it down to the tiniest detail and anticipate any possible problems or roadblocks.

In practice, this meant he would mull over NCC ad copy for days, tinkering with the wording, inserting new ideas or concepts, changing the graphics. Sometimes this meant better ads. More often it meant convoluted ad copy, like the time he wrote a radio ad which combined an attack on Liberal corruption with a warning about election gag laws. It was a confusing mess that ran about 20 seconds too long. He just liked to pack lots of information into a tiny space.

The same thing happened one time with a billboard we wanted to put up attacking forced unionism. Billboard ads have to be simple to be effective. Yet Stephen's proposed wording for the caption was confusing – or at least that's how the staff saw it. I was elected to bite the bullet and express to him our reservations. So I called him up. "Hi Stephen," I said. "We were going over your billboard idea and we think it needs to be changed." Stephen cut me off right there and stated icily, "I don't give a fuck what you think."

Stephen wasn't always that coarse, but there was no question he was the boss and his decisions were final. Stephen liked to call the NCC a "dictatorship fighting for democracy" with him as the dictator. And he didn't take kindly to anyone who challenged his authority.

That's something the guy who ran our telemarketing department learned the hard way. This man, who had been with the NCC since 1988, ran his department like his own petty kingdom. He didn't want anyone – even the NCC president – telling him how to run his shop. He wanted things done his way and he was not shy about letting Stephen know it. How's this for symbolism: when he showed up in our boardroom for staff meetings, he towed along his own leather chair. It was a chair that happened to be fancier and more expensive than Stephen's. Not a good idea. But this guy probably assumed that because he raised a lot of money for the NCC, his job was safe. And if that were the case, he was wrong. Stephen fired him. (No one was sad to see this guy go, as he was an office bully and not well liked.) A couple of days after the firing, Stephen and I wandered into the ex-telemarketing head's office. Stephen looked around for a second and then pointed to the guy's chair and said to me, "Let's burn that."

Dealing with Stephen also meant dealing with his temper. Now by temper, I don't mean he flew into a rage and screamed at the top of his lungs. In fact, in all the years he worked at the NCC I never saw him really lose it, in the sense that he would kick over a chair or throw something. Stephen once bragged to me that he never actually lost his temper. His emotions, he said, were always under control. He simply played the part of an irate boss if he thought instilling fear would yield a desired outcome. Intimidation, in other words, was a calculated tactic. Of course, that didn't make it any more pleasant to endure his wrath. When you were in his bad books you definitely knew about it. And his anger was focused and precise, like a surgical strike. Rather than getting red hot, Stephen got ice cold. If you screwed up, he would meticulously, dispassionately and painstakingly dissect your failure piece by piece, exposing every iota of your incompetence. What's worse, you had to endure his piercingly cold, blue-eyed glare. And his anger, once aroused, would sometimes simmer for weeks.

One thing that would really rile Stephen was sloppy grammar – spelling mistakes, typos, misplaced commas.

It was really a good idea to proofread any written material about ten times before you gave it to him. That's why it's a little ironic that one of his lasting legacies at the NCC is a grammatical error. It has to do with our name. Before Stephen became our president, the official name of the organization was the National Citizens' Coalition, with an apostrophe after "Citizens". That's the grammatically correct spelling. But Stephen just didn't like the apostrophe. He didn't think it looked right. So he decreed it be dropped and we became the National Citizens Coalition, with no apostrophe.

If Stephen was quick to find fault, he was also very slow to offer compliments. He was just not the kind of boss who would slap you on the back and say "Great job!" To him, your paycheque was thanks enough. Needless to say, this didn't make Stephen a great morale booster around the office. My year end performance reviews, for instance, usually went something like this:

Stephen Harper (*face looking grim*): Well Gerry, before we begin your review, let me say you are overpaid for the work you do around here. (That was always his opening gambit to pre-empt me asking for a raise.)

Me: Overpaid? But …

Stephen: Now let's review every single mistake you made over the past year, beginning with that typo I found in a news release you sent out eight months ago …

Me: Sigh

And Stephen was a bit of a workaholic. He worked long hours and expected the same from his staff. Nor did he really believe in vacations or time off. More than once I would get a call from him while I was on holiday, asking me to draft up a new ad campaign or to write an op-ed. One time, on a Friday night when he knew I was at the Skydome watching a baseball game from a friend's Skybox, he called my wife to ask if she knew how to contact me. He wanted me to leave the game early and do some work in our Toronto office. My wife lied and said she couldn't get the number for the box. Another time, when I was home ill, he called to chat and after a few minutes of conversation abruptly declared, "You don't sound sick."

But that was Stephen. He was always suspicious the staff was goofing off. Maybe it's because while he worked in the Calgary office, the rest of us worked three thousand miles away in Toronto. That's why he would do things like stage surprise visits from Calgary, or call the office at 4:55 PM on Friday, just to make sure everybody was there. He even installed surveillance cameras in the office. They were supposedly put in place to record evidence in case the police ever raided our office.

He also abolished the NCC Friday afternoon drinkfest. This was a tradition David started. Every Friday afternoon he and some of his fraternity buddies would gather at the office, along with any NCC employees who wanted to join in, and consume copious amounts of beer. Stephen not only put a stop to that, he also banned alcohol from the premises.

Now, I don't want to give the impression Stephen was a bad boss. Far from it. If you did your work the way he wanted you to, then you could get along with him just fine. Yes, he could be a tough guy, but I don't mind working for tough guys. Besides, in many ways, Stephen helped make the NCC leaner, meaner and more efficient.

Unlike David, who sometimes spent NCC funds a little recklessly, Stephen was much more careful about the NCC's finances. He overhauled our accounting procedures to put the NCC on a sounder footing, and imposed a savage fiscal discipline on the staff. He went through every department with a fine-toothed comb, ruthlessly hacking out anything he deemed wasteful or unnecessary. Nothing made Stephen angrier than waste. Woe to anyone who was even one cent over budget. Unfortunately for the staff, Stephen's austerity program also led him to abolish Christmas bonuses and to freeze salaries. And any business trip meant staying in third-rate hotels.

But Stephen wasn't just good at cost-cutting. He was also a media star. Thanks to the high profile and credibility he earned from his days as a Reform MP, he was a steady guest on radio and TV public affairs programs, his op-eds were picked up in major newspapers and important columnists were always keen to quote him. This was good for the NCC; publicity for Stephen was publicity for us. And it wasn't just that Stephen got lots of media coverage, it was also the way he came across when interviewed. He never seemed flustered. He always knew the right thing to say. No question, no matter how tough, seemed to throw him for a loop. And his knowledge of public policy, economics and fiscal issues was astounding.

All of those positive things aside, it could even be fun to work with Stephen. Contrary to public perception, Stephen is not just an emotionless robot. He is an emotionless robot with a sense of humour. For one thing, he is an excellent mimic. He could do killer impersonations of Joe Clark, Preston Manning and Jean Chrétien. In fact, Stephen actually impersonated Chretien in one of our anti-Liberal radio ads. It was hilarious but, alas, we chickened out and never aired it.

Nor was Stephen simply a policy wonk. When he wasn't discussing politics (which admittedly, he was doing 90 percent of the time) he liked to talk about his favourite TV shows. Those included *Star Trek* (the classic 1960s version – he wanted nothing to do with any of the later Treks) and *Seinfeld,* or about his all-time favourite rock band, the Beatles, or about why cats were obviously superior to dogs.

Everybody on staff also got a kick out of his atrocious eating habits. Now first, let me confess that I am a junk food addict. But even I was shocked at Stephen's dietary choices. He was constantly sneaking out of the office to buy chocolate bars or candies or liquorice sticks. At lunch he would devour gut-bomb burgers and mountains of fries, and drink gallons of pop. Not surprisingly, given his diet, he developed a little bit of a weight problem. This led NCC staffers to give him the secret codename Fatboy, or

FB for short. "Hey," I would write in an email. "You better have that report done before FB comes back." Fortunately, Stephen never found out about that.

But don't let that nickname fool you. I liked Stephen. I respected his keen intellect and his discipline, and never lost confidence in his leadership. I also admired him because he was a man of true conviction. Like NCC founder Colin M. Brown, Stephen had the courage to fight for true conservative values and principles.

I was also grateful to Stephen for the way he expanded my role at the organization. It was Stephen who promoted me from Communications Director to Vice President. It was Stephen who allowed me to write op-eds for the mainstream media under my own name instead of just ghost-writing them. And it was Stephen who gave me the added responsibilities of writing direct mail fundraising letters and editing our online newsletters. Stephen had confidence in me and that helped me believe in myself.

Of course, Stephen and I never became what you would call friends. He always kept a wall between himself and the rest of the staff. But we did form something of a bond. Often, he and I would have long conversations about politics, philosophy and life in general. I really enjoyed those talks and learned a lot. It was during one of those conversations that he told me something a little startling.

Apparently his original plan was to fire me and put one of his own people in the communications job. Luckily for me, he changed his mind. He decided to keep me, he said, because he came to realize that I was "loyal to the core." I took that as a compliment, because I did consider myself loyal. I was loyal to Stephen, but more importantly loyal to the NCC and its values.

CHAPTER 6
THE TEMPTATION OF THE TORIES

B EFORE GOING INTO ANY MORE DETAIL ABOUT STEPHEN'S tenure as NCC president, it's interesting to note that not long after he joined us, he actually came close to leaving us. In fact, he nearly jumped into the Progressive Conservative Party leadership race.

The story behind this little tale began in the spring of 1998, just a few months after Stephen assumed the presidency of the NCC. That's when Jean Charest stepped down as federal PC leader to take over the Quebec Liberal Party. (Only in Canada!)

Almost immediately after it became clear that Charest was leaving federal politics, journalists and pundits started musing about his possible successors. And one name kept popping up again and again: Stephen Harper. And I guess that wasn't really surprising. On paper, Stephen was an ideal candidate. He was young, articulate, bilingual and, prior to his Reform days, a member of the Tory party. And it wasn't just journalists thinking he should take a kick at the Tory can. Stephen confided to me that certain high-level Tories had also been in touch with him, urging him to run.

I didn't take any of this talk seriously. I knew Stephen had no love for the PC party. I knew he believed it was dominated by Red Tories and hence wasn't even truly conservative. (He once said there were two types of Conservatives: Red Tories and Yellow Tories.) But I did sense an opportunity to use all this leadership speculation to the NCC's advantage. After all, the more media pundits bandied Stephen's name around as a possible candidate, the more publicity it would provide the NCC. And as the old adage goes, any publicity is good publicity.

That's why I didn't want Stephen to flat out deny he was running. That would kill the story and end the free media attention. Why not keep it going? Stephen readily agreed with my idea. So our official plan was to keep the media guessing. Whenever questioned about his running for the leadership, we offered non-committal answers. We didn't say he was running, but we didn't say he wasn't. My scheme worked. Speculation about Stephen and the Tories kept bubbling up in the media.

But then something caught me by surprise. On March 27th, the *Globe and Mail* quoted University of Calgary professor Tom Flanagan, who at the time was a close friend and confidante of Stephen, as saying, "Harper could be persuaded to run on a platform of bringing together under one umbrella, the two right of centre parties."

Huh?

That wasn't part of the script. Suddenly questions began to swirl around in my mind. Why was Flanagan speaking for Stephen on this? What was this talk about bringing together the two parties? Then it dawned on me. Maybe Stephen wasn't just playing it coy anymore. Maybe he really did want to run for the leadership of the Tory Party. Could it be?

My suspicions grew on April 7th, when Stephen called to tell me he would soon give an important speech in Calgary to, of all people, the Home and Mortgage Loan Association. He ordered me to alert the media, and informed me that until he gave that speech he would be incommunicado. No media interviews. No leaks. No nothing. That's all I knew.

When I sent out that advisory, the media went crazy. My phone started ringing off the hook with calls from senior journalists – like the CBC's Don Newman and Jason Moscovitz – hounding me for answers, looking for clues. "Was Stephen going to use the speech to announce he was running for the Tories?" "Can he come on my show to talk about the leadership race?" "Will the NCC support his leadership bid?"

The CBC's Parliament Hill reporter, Julie Van Dusen, was particularly persistent. Eager for a scoop, she used every trick in the book to pry a story out of me. "I won't use your name," she promised. "It will be off the record, I'll only use it on background." But I didn't say a word – mainly because I didn't know what Stephen was going to say in that speech.

But one thing I did know is I did not want Stephen to leave us. Maybe it was selfish, but I still had idealistic notions about him leading the NCC to glorious new heights. I didn't want to lose him to the PCs. He had only been with us a year.

The courageous thing to do, of course, would have been to pick up the phone and confront Stephen directly on this issue. So the day before Stephen's scheduled speech, I did pick up the phone and call … our Chairman, Colin T. Brown. (Colin was the son of the NCC's founder.) I shared my concerns with Colin and discovered he was having the same fears. To put it mildly, he was not happy. In fact, he was freaking out. "I am calling Stephen right now to get the bottom of this," he thundered.

I am not sure what Colin said to him, but that night Stephen called me at my home. He told me he was "pulling the plug" on the Tory leadership speculation. He then instructed me to leak this little tidbit to Van Dusen the next morning. I heaved a sigh of relief.

So on April 9th, I called Van Dusen. I can't tell you how much fun it was to have a great bit of gossip to dangle in front of a reporter eager for a scoop. It's a real power trip. I said to her, "Julie, I have news for you." Purposely dragging out the suspense, I paused. "What is it?" she asked, her voice crackling with excitement. "Stephen is not going to run," I declared, using my most solemn voice.

Now it was her turn to pause. "He isn't going to run?" she repeated, as if unable to believe her ears. "Yup, he has decided to stay on as president of the National Citizens Coalition." "Thank you, thank you," she gushed. About an hour later, I watched CBC Newsworld, to see Van Dusen break the story. "Sources close to Harper say he will not seek the leadership of the Conservative Party."

Once Van Dusen's story hit the airwaves, the media calls started pouring in. Some reporters just couldn't believe Stephen wasn't going to throw his hat into the ring. One journalist asked me, "When you say the answer is 'no' is that a real no or a BS no?" "It's a real no, with a capital N and a capital O," I responded, trying to sound as emphatic as I could.

The next day the *Globe and Mail* carried a front page story on Stephen's speech, quoting him as saying he would not be a candidate for the Tory leadership because his "candidacy would burn bridges to those Reformers with whom I worked for many years."[13]

When I saw that story and all the rest of the media fuss, it really struck me for the first time: Stephen was an important political player. He actually could lead a political party, and who knows, maybe even become Prime Minister. Anyway, the Calgary "Burning Bridges Speech" took the wind out of the media's leadership rumour sails.

The *Globe and Mail* even declared Stephen to be "Not Hot" in its "Hot and Not Hot" section. "No one is out there urging the president of the National Citizens Coalition to change his mind and enter the Tory race," wrote the paper.

But Stephen was a little hotter than the *Globe* realized. On April 20th, he was in Toronto and in high spirits. He bounded into my office and said, "Gerry, I am going to an important meeting tomorrow night at 7:00 PM. I want you to be there, too."

The meeting, as it turned out, had nothing to do with NCC business. It had been set up by a group of PC party activists who were still eager for Stephen to run for the leadership of their party. Chief among them was Bob Dechert. A Toronto lawyer and president of the PC Business Association, Dechert was heading up something called the Blue Committee. Its aim was to recruit a right-wing candidate to run against Hugh Segal, a Red Tory who up until that point was the only person in the race to replace Charest. Dechert believed Stephen could be his conservative champion, and Stephen was more than willing to hear him out.

I wasn't the only person Stephen asked to tag along to that meeting. He also asked the NCC's American political consultant and pollster, John McLaughlin. (McLaughlin was a protégé of Arthur Finkelstein.) Stephen had previously discussed the Tory leadership issue with John. And as John later confided to me, those discussions left him convinced of one thing: Stephen definitely wanted to be Prime Minister.

The meeting with the Blue Committee took place in a boardroom in Dechert's downtown law office. In attendance, representing the Blue Committee, were Dechert, Tory MP Jim Jones, a couple of failed Tory candidates from the previous federal election, some kid from the Tory Youth Wing and pollster John Mykytyshyn, a colourful guy who had done work for the Harris Tories.

Throughout the evening, the Blue Committee tried to persuade Stephen to join the leadership race. Each and every person at the table gushed about how Stephen would make the perfect candidate. He was young. He was brilliant. He could speak French. At one point Mykytyshyn piped in, "I know a winner when I see one. And you sir, are a winner." It was all heady stuff. I could see how Stephen might get caught up in it all. When people are lavishing such praise on you, it's hard not to be swayed.

After the meeting wrapped up at about 10:00 PM, Stephen, John and I made our way to a nearby bar to talk it over. Stephen was not impressed. "Did you notice," he said to me, "not once did they ask me where I stood on policy." And Stephen was right. What really seemed to impress the Committee weren't his policy stances. It was that he could speak French. As for John McLaughlin, well, he was all gung-ho and urging Stephen to take the political plunge. "You should do it, you should run," he kept saying.

A week earlier, I would have been kicking John under the table to get him to shut up. But by this time I was thinking maybe Stephen should run for the top Tory job. Maybe I was getting hooked. Maybe it was the excitement of the secret nighttime meetings. Maybe I thought Stephen would make a good prime minister. But maybe, just maybe, I was thinking of my own career. Who knows? If Stephen did run, perhaps he would ask me to be part of his campaign team? How cool would it be to jump into the political big-time and help run a leadership campaign? And if we won? Well the next step might be a national election campaign leading to … leading to what? A job in the Prime Minister's Office perhaps? I could be a front row witness to Canadian history.

At any rate, more and more pressure was mounting on Stephen to become a candidate, and not just from the Blue Committee. Corporate Canada was also getting in on the act. Not long after the Blue Committee meeting, Stephen met with some high-level types from a major public relations firm. According to Stephen, these PR guys urged him to run and offered him professional communications expertise, plus Bay Street endorsements. They also promised to raise lots of cash for his campaign. And just in case Stephen was feeling any guilt about leaving the NCC high and dry, they even offered to take over and run the NCC, lock, stock and barrel.

When I heard about that last part, I wasn't sure what to think. But the rest of it was pretty thrilling. More thrilling news was still to come. Besides the emerging Bay Street support, Stephen also had the backing of some major political guns. And I do mean major. People close to Ontario Premier Mike Harris were also having secret talks with Stephen. They promised to put the powerful Harris political machine at his disposal should he decide to run. All the pieces seemed to be falling into place, all the pieces except for one.

While the support from the Blue Committee and the Harris people and the corporate types was all well and good, Stephen desperately wanted something more, something that wouldn't be easy to get. What Stephen wanted was for some prominent Reformers to endorse his bid for the Tory leadership. That would be hard to get. Yet Stephen seemed cautiously optimistic he could pull it off. He let me know, for instance, that earlier in the year some unnamed Reform MPs had already approached him, urging him to challenge Preston Manning's leadership. Maybe, he reasoned, these same MPs would now endorse his Tory leadership bid. So Stephen started working the phones calling his old Reform colleagues to feel them out on this delicate matter.

His efforts didn't go unnoticed.

In fact, the Reform Party leadership was not amused. And it wasn't long before it struck back. On April 27th, a column entitled, "Harper Making Reform Blood Boil" appeared in the *Calgary Herald*.[14] Written by Peter Menzies, it was explosive stuff. "Spies on Parliament Hill," wrote Menzies, "report the very name of Stephen Harper is causing Reform blood to boil. The former Calgary West MP, who continues to tease and titillate the blue remnants of the federal Tories with a very campy dance of the seven veils, concerning his leadership intentions, is apparently burning up the phone lines to old buddies within the ranks of Preston Manning's caucus."

Later in the piece, Menzies quotes his spies as saying, "Harper's going crazy," and "He wants to run for the Tories, wants to merge them [with Reform] and wants to be the only one left standing." Menzies' Reform sources also claimed Harper was "trying to drive a wedge between the party's fiscal conservatives and its social conservatives. And drive out Manning," whom, Menzies added, Harper "despises." And then there was this quote from one of Menzies' spies: "The NCC logo is a bulldog, not a dog sleeping on a porch."

The real stinger in the piece, however, was this Menzies line: "Harper's actions have undermined his position at the NCC. The latter, it is said, receives a lot of contributions from Reform supporters who dislike being linked to tawdry party politics and shabby politicians at all."

Clearly, somebody in the Reform camp was spinning Menzies and spinning him hard. And Stephen believed it was Ezra Levant, who at the time was working for the Reform Party in Ottawa. It made Stephen furious. He called Levant up the next day to lay down the law. "Don't fuck with me, Ezra," was how he put it.

But there was little Stephen could do to stop a Reform Party assault. Menzies was right about one thing. A large number of NCC supporters were also Reform supporters and that made Stephen somewhat vulnerable. If the Reformers started working on our wealthier supporters, urging them to quit the NCC or to reduce their financial contributions to punish Stephen for his partisan dalliance with the Tories, it could do us some real damage. And that's exactly what Stephen believed was going to happen.

"Make no mistake," he said to me. "The Reform Party is going to wage a war on the NCC and it could get ugly." Stephen was sure the Menzies article was proof the Reform leadership – and more specifically, Preston Manning – was out to stop him from taking over the Tory leadership. At this point, Stephen became moody – something he inevitably did when things were not going his way. And a moody Stephen is a dark Stephen. Not a fun guy to be around.

Before long, he started spinning wild conspiracy theories. One day, he was certain Manning was going to recruit former NCC president David Somerville to undermine him with our Board of Directors. Other times, he was railing about how Manning was ordering Reform MPs to publicly attack him. Not one to take things sitting down, Stephen wanted to hit back. But how? One bizarre scheme Stephen concocted was how he wanted me to write a memo to him about how I believed Manning was trying to destroy Stephen Harper. I was then supposed to leak this memo to the media. How dramatic. How phony!

I refused point blank to do something so ridiculous and the idea was quietly dropped. We also talked about the possibility of running ads praising the Liberal Party, as a way of embarrassing Reformers.

It was all kind of surreal. And it all smacked of Stephen waging some sort of personal vendetta against his old rival, Manning. Of course, I had long known there was ill-feeling between the two of them, but I thought it was just policy that divided them. Stephen once told me he objected to Manning's attempt to dilute the Reform Party's conservative principles. Now, I could see it was also personal, even vindictive. Stephen, in fact, was acting like he did want to drive Manning out. It was during this time that I wrote in my daily journal that he reminded me of "Captain Ahab hunting the white whale."

Meanwhile, Stephen was quietly pondering his political future. As part of that effort, John McLaughlin convinced Arthur Finkelstein to conduct a special poll to assess Stephen's leadership chances. And so it was on June 16th, that Arthur came to Toronto to report on his findings. It was great for me to see Arthur again, but unfortunately for Stephen, the numbers were not great. The upshot: Stephen was a star in the world of media and politics, but to most Canadian voters he was still largely unknown. His name recognition was next to nil. Not a good sign for somebody who wanted to become Prime Minister. Because of that poll and because he failed to win any support from within the Reform Party, Stephen dropped out of a leadership race he had never officially entered.

His political career was back on hold. It was time for him to concentrate on NCC business again, at least for a while.

Chapter 7
The NCC Gets Wonkier

WITH HIS TORY FLIRTATION OVER, STEPHEN COULD now focus on running the NCC. A task he took on with gusto. In fact, not long after assuming the group's presidency, he was promising "radical changes."

And one of those changes was to revamp the NCC's image. He wanted the NCC to engage in less political theatre and to focus on more serious, substantive issues. In other words, Stephen wanted less sizzle and more steak.

This sometimes led to creative tension between us; a clash of contrasting styles. While he was pontificating about Hayek or Von Mises, I was figuring out ways to compare politicians to various barnyard animals. Still, I also realized the NCC had always more or less reflected the personality of its leaders. Colin M. Brown was a scrappy populist. David Somerville was a flamboyant, bomb-thrower. And Stephen ... well Stephen was a brainy, policy wonk. So when he became our leader, inevitability the NCC would get a little brainier and a little policy wonkier.

What did that mean in practical terms? Well, for one thing, it meant the NCC became less of an agitator and more of a litigator. In other words, Stephen wanted to get away from flashy issue-oriented ad campaigns and focus more on advancing our agenda through strategic court challenges. Unlike many Canadian conservatives who distrust our court system and its "activist" judges, Stephen believed conservatives could and should use the Charter of Rights and Freedoms to promote a freedom agenda, just as the Left was using it to promote activist government.

He once noted, for instance, how the NCC had used the courts to overturn election gag laws. "Only through court rulings," he wrote in a *Globe and Mail* op-ed, "have these provisions been exposed for what they are: arbitrary and unconstitutional provisions that confer advantages to the major parties at the expense of potential competitors and citizens' fundamental freedoms. It has only been through the courts that the famed 'democratic legitimacy' of our elections has been preserved. In short, the judges' activism is not resolved by the politicians' supremacy. Solutions can only be found in the classical theory of liberal democracy – checks and balances of institutional power under limited government. Unfortunately, this is something neither our Charter nor our Parliament provides."[15]

And the NCC was no stranger to court battles. We had turned to the courts to fight for freedom in both the Merv Lavigne case and in the gag law challenges. But under Stephen we found ourselves in more courtrooms fighting more battles.

Here's a rundown of those court fights:

THE FUDGET-BUDGET

A British Columbian businessman named David Stockell had set up a group called HELP BC, which was an acronym for Help Eliminate Lying Politicians. Why had he done that? Well, it was because during BC's 1996 provincial election, the NDP, under then Premier Glen Clark, had bragged about their fiscal management in balancing the province's budget. It was a key part of their re-election campaign and likely helped the NDP win that election. However, after the election was over, some disturbing news emerged. It turned out the NDP had not really balanced the budget after all. In fact, the province was actually in deficit. What's more, it seems the NDP knew during the election that they were in a deficit. Had the NDP purposely misled voters about the budget to win the election? That's what Stockell believed. To be blunt, he believed the NDP had lied. After checking out BC's election laws, he discovered that, if the NDP did lie, they might actually have broken the law. Section 156 of the BC Election Act says, "An individual or organization must not by abduction, duress or fraudulent means ... compel, persuade or otherwise cause an individual to vote or refrain from voting for a particular candidate or a particular political party."

To Stockell, lying to the public was the same as using "fraudulent means" to persuade voters. So he decided to sue the NDP. As a first step, he set up HELP BC. Then he ran some newspaper ads which helped him find three voters who said they had been duped into voting NDP and who were willing to take their local NDP MLAs to court for fraud. All Stockell needed now was money. And that's where the NCC came into the picture.

Originally, it was David Somerville who contacted Stockell and offered him the NCC's financial aid, but Stephen took on the case with a passion. He even absorbed HELP BC into the NCC and hired Stockell as a vice president. For Stephen, this was an extremely important court battle. It was about political accountability. Shouldn't politicians tell the truth during elections? If they do lie, isn't that fraud? And if lying is the same as fraud, shouldn't citizens be allowed to seek redress in the courts?

Certainly this case had important implications for BC's NDP government. If the BC courts did rule the NDP had committed electoral fraud, then three NDP MLAs could have been removed from office and maybe even sent to jail. This would have reduced the NDP majority to one seat. But Stephen was thinking beyond just BC. He was hoping this court case would lead citizens in other provinces to demand their election laws be amended to make lying during elections a crime. That's why the NCC used its resources to make this fraud challenge a national issue. One of our newspaper ads had a caricature of Clark under the headline, "Fit to be Tried."

Personally, I didn't think this case had much chance of success. It was just too much to expect judges would have the courage to interpret "fraudulent means" as including political lying. As one of the lawyers in the case noted, "If a candidate has made a knowingly false promise during a campaign, every election would be susceptible to challenge." That's why I assumed the courts would dismiss this case in its early stages. But I was wrong. The courts kept rejecting early procedural attempts by the NDP to have the case thrown out. This was such an unusual, unprecedented challenge that even the judges didn't quite know what to make of it. As one judge declared during the proceedings, "We're making this up as we go along." Hence, this case actually made it to trial in 2000.

Alas on August 3rd, 2000, Justice Mary Humphries of the BC Supreme Court dismissed the fraud charges. She ruled that there was no fraud because budgets are just financial forecasts that can turn out to be wrong. It seemed an odd ruling because the NDP government did not promise to balance the budget. It said it had balanced the budget. That's a big difference. But although we lost the case, the challenge received a lot of publicity, both in BC and around the country. It became known as the Fudget-budget scandal. This, in turn, proved quite embarrassing for the NDP and likely played a role in the party's collapse in the 2001 provincial election.

ELECTION BLACKOUT LAWS

On Election Day 2000, a British Columbia computer software developer named Paul Bryan posted real-time election results from Atlantic Canada on his website.

He didn't project winners. He just posted raw voting information so Canadians who were interested could see what was going on. It seemed like a harmless act. In fact, any Canadian with Internet access could have found the same information that night on the websites of news organizations such as CNN, Yahoo and ABC News.

In fact, Bryan, in posting those results, was purposely violating the law. Section 329 of the Canada Elections Act, which was enacted in 1938, bans what's officially called the "premature transmission" of voting results on election night. Under this law it's a crime to let Canadians living in parts of the country where the polls are still open know what the election results are in parts of the country where the polls are closed. Essentially, Section 329 is a blackout law or, to put it less delicately, censorship. Can such election censorship be justified in a free and democratic society?

Paul Bryan didn't think so. He believed Section 329 was an infringement on his Charter-guaranteed right to free expression. He also believed it was wrong to ban the free flow of political information on election night or any other night for that matter. In addition, he didn't think blackout laws even made sense – or were enforceable – in this age of the Internet and satellite communication.

Communications technology, after all, has come a long way since 1938. We now live in an era of instantaneous, easily accessible information, meaning government simply cannot keep information under wraps the way it once did.

As Paul put it, "People can beam around information worldwide in micro-seconds, and government wants to ban our use of it when it becomes inconvenient. It's time for the Canadian government to join the rest of us in the 21st century." That's why he purposely violated the law. He wanted to be charged so he could convince the courts to scrap what he considered an election gag law.

And he wasn't disappointed. Within two weeks of election night, Elections Canada officials, assisted by the RCMP, went to Bryan's home to search his files and computer equipment. They seized his computer hard drives and credit card statements. Then, a few months later, Bryan was officially charged with violating the law, meaning he faced a fine of up to $25,000.

When Stephen found about this case he was impressed with Bryan's courage and determination to stand up for free expression. Accordingly, he offered to help pay for Bryan's legal expenses. To Stephen this was about more than just fighting a blackout law. He was concerned about politicians and bureaucrats stifling free speech on what was then a new communications tool – the Internet. As Stephen himself wrote in a letter to NCC supporters, "We can't allow the government to dictate what information we can or cannot publish. We can't allow them to seize control of the Internet – new technology that promises to revolutionize politics. And we can't allow them to ruin a principled citizen who has the guts to stand up for what he believes in."

And this was one case where the media was definitely on our side. Several media outlets, including the CBC, CTV, Sun Media, the Canadian Press, Rogers Broadcasting, CanWest and the *Globe and Mail,* eventually intervened in this case to support Bryan's challenge. It's not hard to see why. Journalists are paid to disseminate information, not suppress it. Yet Section 329 essentially forces the media to censor themselves every election night. That's something no journalist likes to do.

In 2003, Bryan won a major victory when the British Columbia Supreme Court ruled Section 329 did violate the Charter-guaranteed right to free expression. And although that ruling just concerned BC, Elections Canada decided to lift the ban for the entire country. That meant on election night 2004, the media was free to transmit real-time voting results without fear of the blackout rules. However, that turned out to be a brief respite. For in May 2005, the BC Court of Appeal reversed the lower court ruling. Then, in March 2007, the Supreme Court of Canada, in a close five to four ruling, also declared the blackout law to be constitutional.

The Supreme Court apparently didn't care that section 329 infringed on free speech. Why? Because they believed it was a necessary infringement to safeguard what one

Justice called "informational equality." Yes, apparently "informational equality" is an important right, more important even than the right to free speech, which just happens to be entrenched in the Charter.

TAKING ON THE LITTLE KREMLIN ON THE PRAIRIE

If there is one thing Stephen didn't like it was the Canadian Wheat Board. More precisely, he didn't like the Board's monopoly. And he had every reason not to like it. The Board monopoly is an archaic, oppressive, government-created marketing scheme that combines the worst elements of socialism, feudalism and bureaucratic stupidity. The way the monopoly works is that western grain farmers are forced to sell nearly all their crops to the Canadian Wheat Board, whether they want to or not. It's grain management, Joseph Stalin-style. Stephen saw this monopoly as a serious infringement on the economic and democratic rights of farmers. Shouldn't western grain farmers have the right to sell their own crops to customers of their own choice? Grain farmers in other parts of Canada had that right. As Stephen noted in an NCC news release, "It's long past time to scrap the monopoly and restore freedom to farmers."

Of course, the NCC was adamantly opposed to the Wheat Board monopoly before Stephen came along. In the mid-1990s, the NCC had offered financial help to a number of pro-free market western farmers who were fighting the monopoly with media campaigns. But Stephen also wanted to take the case against the Wheat Board to the courts. Consequently, the NCC teamed up with a remarkable farmer named Dave Bryan, who was ready and eager to challenge the Board's monopoly.

In 1996 Bryan had been charged with exporting barley to the United States without a license, which violated the Canada Wheat Board Act. Bryan readily admitted his guilt. He wanted to use his case to put the Wheat Board monopoly on trial. As he wrote, "Sometimes it's necessary and right for good people to willingly go to jail to expose an injustice."

His case centered on the question of property rights. When a farmer grows grain, Bryan argued, it's his property and he should have the right to sell his property to whatever customer he chooses. Although property rights are not enshrined in the Charter, Bryan noted that they were protected under the Bill of Rights. What's more, Bryan questioned the constitutionality of the federal government's right to regulate property. That is supposed to be provincial jurisdiction. As Stephen noted in a news release, Bryan's case "goes right to the heart of property rights and the federal government's unresolved jurisdiction."

Unfortunately, the Manitoba courts dismissed Bryan's claims. It seems the question of private property rights didn't much concern them. As the Manitoba Court of Appeal put it, in their 1999 ruling, " ... the right to 'enjoyment of property' is not a constitutionally protected, fundamental part of Canadian society." It was a ruling that stunned advocates of private property rights. Danielle Smith, then head of the Calgary-based Canadian Property Rights Research Institute, called the ruling "extremely alarming" and "chilling" and noted that " it openly states what we've known all along: there is no secure protection for property rights in Canadian law."[16] And Smith added, "Isn't it a shame that, with one brush stroke, you can destroy 700 years of the British Common Law tradition and the institutions we've built Canadian society on.'"

A shame, indeed! In the early 1980s, the NCC had pushed our leaders to include the right to own private property in the constitution. This ruling showed why we did.

One benefit of having Stephen as NCC president, was that he opened up a line of communication to Quebec, a province where we had little representation. It wasn't just that Stephen could speak fluent French, but that he had contacts with Quebec's small but vibrant libertarian community. One of those contacts was crusading lawyer Brent Tyler.

Tyler is something of a civil-rights hero who has made it his life's mission to legally challenge Quebec's anti-English language laws. Tyler believes Quebec Anglophones have sacrificed their rights for too long in the name of Canadian unity and "language peace." He wants to fight for what's right. That attitude appealed to Stephen, who, like Tyler, viewed Quebec's language laws as draconian. So the NCC offered to help subsidize some of Tyler's legal challenges.

Specifically, the NCC helped to finance two of Tyler's court battles. One case involved the owners of an antique shop called "The Wallrus and Lyon", located in the Eastern Townships. The owners, Gwen Simpson and Wally Hoffman, were charged and fined $500 by Quebec's language cops because the English and French lettering on their sign were the same size. Under Quebec's Bill 86, French must be predominant.

Tyler took on their case and initially, was successful. In 1999 a Quebec court ruled the province couldn't continue to impose restrictions on the use of languages other than

French on commercial signs, unless it could prove the fragility of the French language in Quebec society.

That ruling caught people by surprise and predictably triggered outrage among Quebec's nationalists. Even the provincial Liberals, under Jean Charest, were angered. Charest went so far as to accuse the Parti Quebecois government of losing the case on purpose to provoke a language crisis. "It looks like a provocation," declared Charest. "It is either provocation – or incompetence at the highest level."[17]

As it turns out, Charest didn't have to worry. In 2000, the Quebec Superior Count overturned the 1999 ruling.

The other case involved francophone parents who wanted the right to send their children to English-speaking public schools. Tyler argued they had this right under section 23(2) of the Charter of Rights and Freedoms, which protects educational equality. This case eventually went to the Supreme Court of Canada, where unfortunately, in 2005, Tyler lost. Essentially, the Supreme Court ruled that it was okay for Quebec to prohibit French-speaking students from receiving an English-language education. As the court put it, "Equality rights, while of immense importance, constitute just part of our constitutional fabric. Language education rights cannot be subordinated to the equality rights guarantees."

The NCC support for Tyler created something of a stir among Quebec nationalists. They thought it improper that a group largely based outside of Quebec should be financing a court challenge to the province's language laws.

As one Quebec government official put it, (translation) "It's certainly debatable that one is financing from outside Quebec a case which put into question the French Language Charter, which is one of Quebec's most fundamental institutions."[18]

Besides becoming more involved in court battles, Stephen also wanted the NCC to be a little kinder and gentler. To soften our image a bit, he changed the name of our newsletter from the aggressive-sounding *The Bulldog,* to the more serene-sounding *Freedom Watch.* And he never liked the belligerent way the NCC had gone after politicians in the past. He felt they were "personal attacks." Again, this sometimes led to a clash of styles between me and Stephen. As an Arthur Finkelstein-trained political warrior, I was constantly pushing for tough, hard-edged campaigns. I was then, and am now, a big proponent of what some call negative advertising. I like negative advertising for one simple reason: it works. As famed Liberal attack dog Warren Kinsella wrote, in *Kicking Ass in Canadian Politics,* "Political types say they don't like doing the tough stuff – but they do. And voters say they aren't influenced by tough stuff – but they are."[19] Also, I might add, negative ads are fun to write.

One time, I wanted to go after Liberal MP Ralph Goodale and punish him for his support of the Canadian Wheat

Board monopoly. So I came up with a Rile Ralph Day campaign which would have involved a one day anti-Goodale ad blitz. And yes, it probably would have qualified as negative campaigning. It was, in short, an old-fashioned NCC sort of idea. But it never saw the light of day. Stephen hated it.

Nor did he like our famous NCC pigs, the ones we had used so successfully in our ads exposing government waste and opposing MP pensions. He actually wanted to retire them from our arsenal. Fortunately, I talked him out of that drastic move by explaining how much our supporters and the media loved our cute little pigs.

Overall, I was fairly successful in my efforts to keep the NCC from becoming too intellectual. It took a lot of persuading on my part, but I eventually convinced Stephen that good advocacy meant imaginative messaging. And so, while our ads may have lacked the punch of pre-Harper days, they were still fun and they still had an impact.

For instance, to expose how union bosses were using forced dues to finance an anti-Mike Harris ad campaign, I created a radio ad spot called Forced Dues Blues. It included a nifty blues music soundtrack and an announcer warning about how "big union bosses were giving workers a bad case of the blues."

As part of our anti-Wheat Board campaign, I put up a billboard in Regina, near the office of Ralph Goodale, with a caption reading, "End the Wheat Board Monopoly,

Goodale. Selling Wheat Shouldn't Be A Crime." To emphasize the point, the "o"s in the word "Goodale" were portrayed as handcuffs.

So while Stephen was making the NCC a little kinder, I was ensuring it wasn't much gentler.

Still, one thing about the NCC definitely changed when Stephen took over and that was our relationship with the media. When David Somerville was NCC president, his theory about media relations was simple: get in the media's face as much as you can, flood the market with news releases, send them to every media outlet on the planet. Stephen, on the other hand, had a different philosophy. He thought sending out news releases didn't accomplish much, especially when sent out in a shotgun pattern. So when he assumed control, the NCC sent out fewer news releases and, when we did send them, they were often only sent to selected journalists. It was the same for news conferences. Under David, the NCC held several news conferences a year in Toronto, Ottawa and Calgary. By contrast, during Stephen's four years as president, the NCC held only one.

Stephen's approach to the media was more personal. When he wanted to get a story out he would simply contact a journalist he trusted or respected and give it to him or her directly. He also didn't like to do taped TV interviews, preferring to appear live on programs like *Politics* on CBC's Newsworld, where he appeared regularly as part of a pundit panel.

For Stephen it was all about control. He didn't trust the media to get our message out. And he believed it was a mistake to get too friendly with the press. As he once explained to me, the secret to dealing with the Ottawa press corps was to copy Pierre Trudeau's approach. "Trudeau," he said, "treated reporters with contempt and yet they worshipped him."

Stephen also had a grandiose scheme in the works to establish a sort of Canada-wide conservative empire, with the NCC at the top overseeing a series of satellite groups. In Quebec, he wanted to set up the United Canada Network as a pro-federalist, English language-rights activist group. In Ontario, our project group, Ontarians for Responsible Government, would take on the role of pushing the Harris government into privatizing government agencies and promoting school choice. In Western Canada, he wanted to create a pro-free market farmer group to oppose the Wheat Board monopoly. Meanwhile, he hoped HELP BC would morph into a provincial version of the NCC. (That didn't happen, as David Stockell quit the NCC soon after the fraud case ruling.) He also provided seed money to help establish Labourwatch, an organization which would both promote the rights of unionized employees and expose the undemocratic practices of Canada's union bosses. At one point, he even entered into talks about a possible merger with the Canadian Taxpayers Federation.

Now, these moves on Stephen's part were not about NCC imperialism, but about the NCC's survival. Stephen believed the NCC had to expand or it would die. And he was right. In fact, by the time Stephen took over the NCC, the organization was facing serious problems.

For one thing – and this might sound strange – we were running out of bad guys to fight. And that's a big deal because advocacy groups like the NCC need bad guys. We need somebody we can point to and say, "Hey, there is a scary guy out there whose policies are going to hurt you. Send us money." It's like Brian Mulroney once said, "In politics, you need two things: friends, but above all an enemy." Pierre Trudeau was a good enemy for us. Ed Broadbent was a good enemy. And Bob Rae was the best enemy we ever had. Basically, all I had to do was write letters to people saying, "We want to dump Bob Rae," and they would send me back bucketfuls of money.

However, by 1999, Rae was but a distant memory. His replacement, Premier Mike Harris, was a good guy who was implementing an NCC-style pro-free market agenda. Meanwhile even the federal Liberals, under Prime Minister Jean Chrétien, were acting in a more or less fiscally responsible manner, balancing the federal budget and cutting taxes. So the bottom line was that the NCC had less and less to bitch about. In a sense, we were a victim of our own success in pushing for better government. And while that was good news for the country, it also made it more difficult to raise funds.

What's more, the NCC was facing increasing competition for scarce donation dollars. Gone were the days when the NCC was the only game in town when it came to conservative activism, when we more or less had the market cornered. We were now competing for both media attention and for financial donations with the conservative-oriented Reform Party (later Canadian Alliance) and with upstart groups like the increasingly aggressive Canadian Taxpayers Federation.

Our most serious dilemma, however, was that our membership list was dwindling. This was not because we were doing anything wrong. It's just that a large chunk of our membership base belonged to the World War II generation. And sadly, they were dying off. Unless we could do something to attract new supporters, the NCC would eventually fade away.

That was a long-term problem. But Stephen first had to face a more immediate threat. In 2000, the Liberal government enacted a brand new election gag law. No doubt still stinging from the NCC's 1997 Operation Pork Chop campaign, the Liberals were once again seeking to stifle our right to free speech during elections.

This time, it was Jean Chrétien doing the stifling. Like Trudeau and Mulroney before him, Chrétien imposed a gag law which would severely limit how much money citizens or groups could spend on election advertising. Admittedly, they were higher limits than before. Chrétien's law allowed non-politicians to spend $150,000 on national election advertising and $3000 on ads in local ridings. But that still amounted to a ban on *effective* election speech.

It's impossible to run an effective national ad campaign for only $150,000. And the $3,000 local limit is such an absurdly low amount, it's essentially a total ban on paid election speech.

In other ways, Chrétien's gag law was actually worse than its predecessors. The two previous gag laws, for instance, strictly defined election advertising as any ad that supported or opposed a political candidate or party. Chrétien's gag law went beyond that. Under his gag law election advertising was defined as any ad taking a stand on any issue *associated* with any party or candidate. In other words, Chrétien's gag law made it a crime to run effective election ad campaigns denouncing or endorsing issues like the Kyoto Accord, or the gun registry program, or abortion laws, or trade treaties or virtually any other issue.

Finally, Chrétien's gag law required anyone spending more than $500 on election advertising to register with Elections Canada. This was a process that was costly, burdensome and intrusive. And here's the scary part: nothing in the gag law said the Chief Electoral officer had to accept your registration. If your registration was refused, it meant you couldn't speak out. Our freedom of speech now depended on the whim of a bureaucrat.

To be blunt, this gag law was the most dangerous assault on free political expression in Canada's history.

And the NCC was ready to wage war against it. No sooner had the gag law been enacted than Stephen announced we would launch a court challenge to have it overturned. Make no mistake, Stephen detested the gag law. He even told the media that if he had to, he would purposely flout the law and risk imprisonment.

On the bright side, this gag law fight provided us with two good enemies: an old one and a new one. The old one was our long-time foe Chrétien, the new one Chief Electoral Officer Jean Pierre Kingsley. Not to put too fine a point on it, but Stephen despised Kingsley, whom he contemptuously referred to as "that bald-headed bureaucrat."

In fact, for us, Kingsley was actually a bigger gag law villain than Chrétien. Kingsley, after all, was no mere disinterested bureaucrat. Rather, he was a vocal proponent of gag laws who had vigorously lobbied the government to enact legal restrictions on free speech. He was, in short, a gag law zealot.

And even Stephen "I don't believe in personal attacks" Harper couldn't resist taking shots at this guy. In a letter to raise funds for our challenge to the Election blackout laws, Stephen wrote,

"The jackasses at Elections Canada are out of control." He also called Kingsley a "dangerous man" who was using "iron-fisted bully tactics." These were tough words with which I couldn't disagree.

By the end of 2000, however, our gag law fight was taking a back seat to another issue of extreme importance to Stephen – the role of Alberta in Canada's Confederation. Although he was born in Ontario, Stephen had moved to Alberta as a young man and he was proud of his adopted province's values and culture. At the same time, he was coming to resent what he considered an anti-Alberta bias in Eastern Canada.

This bias reared its ugly head during the 2000 federal election, when not only did Prime Minister Jean Chrétien make anti-Alberta comments, but he derisively slurred Albertans by calling them a "different type" of Canadians. Stephen wrote at the time that Chrétien "seems intent on winning in the East by demonizing the West, Alberta in particular. There is real anger here about his blatantly untruthful, anti-Alberta healthcare ads. Since there are more Easterners than Westerners … the Liberals will win this election. But what does it say about the long-run future of the country? Sorry, folks, but out here it's getting hard to feel you're part of one country."[20]

Of course, not only did the Liberals win that election, but they nearly swept the entire province of Ontario, winning 101 out of a possible 103 seats. A couple of days after the election, Stephen called me from Calgary and he was in a black mood. Ontarians, he told me, didn't reject the Canadian Alliance, they rejected Alberta and its values. He was livid. And it was this anger which led him and other Alberta intellectuals to author the infamous Firewall letter to Alberta Premier Ralph Klein.

Stephen was calling upon Klein to implement an "Alberta Agenda." This agenda would be about Albertans asserting more control over areas already in their constitutional jurisdiction: creating an Alberta pension plan, collecting a provincial income tax, setting up a provincial police force. Only by erecting a firewall, argued Stephen, could Albertans protect their values and resources from an unfriendly and potentially rapacious federal government.

This letter was published in the *National Post* in January 2001, and almost immediately Stephen came under criticism for supposedly espousing an Albertan brand of separatism. But that was not what he was doing. A few weeks before the firewall letter became public, he and I talked about his plans over lunch.

What he wanted to do was have the NCC set up an Alberta nationalist group called the Alberta Citizens Coalition, the sole function of which would be to promote and publicize the Alberta Agenda. Things on this front actually got rolling in early 2001, when the NCC ran a media ad campaign during Alberta's provincial election warning Albertans about "Chrétien's tough love agenda" to control the province's resources.

In a news release to announce the ad blitz, Stephen explained, "We believe Albertans will have two choices in this provincial election. They can vote for the Liberals or they can vote for Alberta. We want Albertans to vote for Alberta. That's the message we plan to hammer home in the weeks ahead on radio, on TV, and in newspapers. As we say in our radio ad, if Albertans vote Liberal, Chrétien will take it as a green light to take more Alberta money for more federal boondoggles. Simply put, a vote for a Liberal candidate in this election is a vote for Chrétien."

The NCC radio ads in that campaign ended with this tag line, "Alberta needs an Alberta Agenda, not a Chrétien agenda."

Looking ahead to the long-term, Stephen also wanted the Alberta Citizens Coalition to perhaps form the nucleus of a new Alberta political party. And who would lead that party? Stephen Harper would, of course. So just like in 1998 when the Tories came calling, Stephen was once again pondering a return to partisan politics. But now he was thinking provincial, not federal.

All of this convinced me that Stephen could very well be the next Premier of Alberta.

Yet only a few months later Stephen had a change of plans.

CHAPTER 8
THE CANADIAN ALLIANCE
COMES CALLING

BY APRIL 2001, CANADIAN ALLIANCE leader STOCKWELL Day was in deep trouble. Polls showed that among Canadians he was about as popular as Canadian flags at a Bloc Quebecois convention. And even his own caucus – fed up with Day's incompetence, poor judgment and political blunders – was erupting into open rebellion, with some CA MPs calling upon him to resign.

I knew if Day did go belly up, Stephen would be under tremendous pressure to replace him as leader. Indeed, as early as February, Stephen told me Alliance MPs were on his case, pushing him to rescue the party. Of course, the same thing happened a year earlier when people were pushing him to take on Preston Manning in the Alliance's first-ever leadership race. At that time, however, Stephen wanted nothing to do with the Alliance, the creation of which he opposed from the very beginning. Stephen feared the Alliance would be more like a Manning personality cult than an agenda-driven, principled conservative party.

Indeed, in 1999, when Manning first proposed the idea of replacing the Reform Party with some sort of united alternative, Stephen told me he was going to wage "guerrilla warfare" to try and stop it. And he did wage such a war. The NCC spent $20,000 to commission a poll which showed Reformers were deeply divided about morphing their party into a new entity. As Stephen told the media, "These results confirm that the Reform/UA has become a house divided against itself."[21] We released that poll just a few days before Reformers and breakaway Tories were to hold a convention on the question of forming a new party. It was a move which the *Globe and Mail* likened to throwing a "grenade into Preston Manning's camp."[22]

And so, given Stephen's antagonism to the project, it's not surprising that when the Canadian Alliance was officially created, he opted to keep his distance. Nevertheless, he did endorse Tom Long, who was a candidate for the new party's leadership.

By mid-2001, however, the political situation had changed. The Canadian Alliance was in terrible shape and Stephen was growing increasingly pessimistic about its future. He believed the Alliance was on the verge of complete collapse. And if the Alliance went under, it would mean the Joe Clark-led Red Tories would be the only alternative to the Liberals, meaning Canada's last hope for a truly conservative voice would be gone.

The Alliance needed a new leader. It needed a new champion. It needed Stephen Harper. So I wasn't all that surprised when, on June 7th he gave me some important news: he was leaving the NCC. "Maybe I will seek the leadership of the Canadian Alliance or maybe I won't," he said. "I am not really sure. But either way, I will be quitting the NCC within the year."

Of course, I knew he was going back into partisan politics. He had to. But still I tried to talk him out of it. It's not that I didn't think he could win the leadership of the Alliance. The question I had to ask him was, "Why would you want to?" He replied, "Because I don't want my kids to grow up in a socialist country." How could I argue with that?

Needless to say, this was all supposed to be hush-hush. Stephen didn't want to talk to the media about Day's problems, or about the Alliance or about his political future. So we went over, in great detail, what I was supposed to tell any journalist inquiring about his leadership ambitions. When asked about Stephen's view of the Canadian Alliance, I would reply, "Mr. Harper is occupied with his work for the organization and it's too soon to comment. He might have some comment when the leadership situation is clarified."

On the other hand, others were speculating quite openly about Harper and the Alliance. Former CA MP Ian McLelland, for instance, went so far as to tell the media that he was busy laying the groundwork for a Harper leadership campaign.[23]

The next time I talked to Stephen about Alliance stuff was in July. He told me he had a meeting in Calgary with Stockwell Day, who, according to Stephen, was an "emotional wreck" and set to resign his post. Stephen talked him out of it, convincing Day to instead call for a leadership race. By this time, Stephen was devoting all of his energy preparing for that race. For all intents and purposes, he was no longer NCC president. He held a staff meeting on July 24th to inform us he was withdrawing from the day to day operations of the organization so he could concentrate on exploring his possible return to federal politics.

At the same time, he appointed Mark Kihn as his unofficial replacement. Stephen had hired Mark in 1999 to write and edit the NCC's newsletters. A genial Calgarian, Mark was a good friend of Stephen's and prior to working for the NCC, he had been the editor of a cattle magazine. And while I am sure Mark was an expert on bull semen and cow breeding, he knew very little about politics or advocacy or fundraising. Mark was, however, completely and utterly loyal to Stephen, a fact which became more than clear in the months ahead.

But I am getting ahead of myself.

After Stephen's unofficial retirement from the NCC in July, I didn't hear from him again for a few weeks. Then, on the morning of August 13th, he sent me an email. The message was short and sweet. "Gerry, send out a media advisory saying the following: Stephen Harper has informed

National Citizens Coalition Chairman Colin Brown that he intends to leave the presidency of the NCC no later than December 31."

So now it was official. He was really leaving us. The next day he called me to confirm the obvious. He was going to seek the Alliance leadership, although I wasn't supposed to spoil the surprise and tell the media.

Not long after that announcement, the NCC sent out its own news release to comment on Stephen's departure. "We are very sad to lose Stephen as President," stated our Chairman Colin Brown Jr. "His leadership skills, his good judgment, and his strong commitment to freedom made him the ideal person to lead the NCC in its fight for 'more freedom through less government.' We wish Stephen the best of luck in whatever course he decides to take and we shall certainly value his continuing contributions to our organization."

Colin went on to say, "Stephen told me that it was an honour and privilege for him to serve the NCC supporters, whom he called a remarkable group of Canadians, and to lead a movement that fights for the values he deeply believes in."

After that he more or less disappeared again, taking no part in the running of the NCC – with one exception. After the 9/11 terrorist attacks, he shot down my plan to put up a billboard showing an American and Canadian flag flying side by side, over the caption "Together for Freedom." He said it wasn't part of the NCC's mandate. I appealed that decision to our chairman, Colin Brown Jr., (who is half-American) and he overruled Stephen and gave me the go ahead to put up the billboard. It turned out to be one of most popular media campaigns in the NCC's history.

On November 27th, Stephen, who was set to officially announce his candidacy for the CA leadership a few days later, showed up at the Toronto office for the last time as NCC president. And he didn't really look like Stephen. Instead of the usual suit, he was wearing jeans, a plaid shirt and had on his glasses, which he hardly ever wore. He also looked like a guy who had just returned from his mother's funeral. I had never seen him look so somber. To cheer him up, I gave him a little pep talk. "This is going to be a great adventure Stephen. This is an exciting time for you." But it was no use. He was clearly not looking forward to what lay in store for him. We chatted for about an hour or so, and then he said good-bye and left. And "goodbye" was about the extent of his farewell. There was no "It was great working with you," no "Thanks for all you did for me during the last four years," no "I am going to miss you guys," no nothing. He just walked out.

But although he was no longer part of the NCC family, Stephen was still with us in spirit – actually more than in spirit. Mark Kihn saw to that. Mark was actually wearing two hats. He was the Executive Vice President of the National Citizens Coalition and he was also the chief fundraiser for the Harper Leadership Campaign.

It's difficult to serve two masters, so maybe that's why Mark opted to serve just one: Stephen Harper. In fact, he quickly turned the NCC into an adjunct of the Harper leadership machine. Suddenly our newsletters were magically transformed into Harper propaganda pieces. Suddenly Harper fundraising mailings were taking precedence over NCC mailings. And suddenly Harper volunteers were swarming all over our office, stuffing envelopes and using our postage machine. None of this was good.

The NCC had no business helping Harper in any way, ex-president or not. We were supposed to be non-partisan. In fact, NCC staff members were even prohibited from belonging to any political party.

The worst part of it all, however, was that I went along with it. Indeed, not only did I go along with it, I actively participated. Starting in October, I started writing fundraising letters for the Harper campaign. And they were good letters too – if I do say so myself – masterpieces even. Here's an excerpt from the first letter I wrote, which went out over the signature of Stephen's campaign manager, Tom Flanagan:

> *Imagine the Canadian Alliance didn't exit. Imagine if no political party spoke for Canadians like you who cherish conservative principles and values. Imagine the only alternative to Jean Chrétien's arrogant, spend-happy Liberals were Joe Clark's arrogant, spend-happy Red Tories. Not a pretty picture is it? Of course, I know you don't want the Canadian Alliance and its principles to disappear.*

That's why you stayed loyal when others deserted the Party. When the left-wing media declared the Alliance was dead, you held firm. I know it hasn't been easy … But here's the good news. You've finally got somebody fighting on your side!

The letter was a smash hit. It raised the Harper campaign more than $400,000[24].

Mark asked me to write a second letter which I made even more emotional than the first:

You know Stephen. Maybe you remember him from the days when he was one of the Reform Party's most effective and energetic MPs. You may even recall he was founder of the Reform Party and was its first chief policy officer. You may recognize him as a principal author of Reform's original "Blue Book." You might remember all that because you were once a strong supporter of the Reform Party. Then something happened. You became disillusioned. The party lost your trust. Perhaps, like many others, you came to believe the party had lost its direction, that it had turned its back on the principles and values you cherish. But I hope the spirit which led you to originally join the Reform Party is still alive inside you. The spirit that gives you the strength and courage to fight for what's right. That same spirit also burns inside Stephen Harper. It's the spirit of a true conservative – a true reformer.

That letter raised more than $200,000.[25]

I was then asked to write a third letter, then a fourth. All told, my direct mail pieces garnered Stephen nearly $1 million.[26] In other words, thanks to my efforts and my letters, the Harper team didn't have to worry about money. And besides writing direct mail pieces, I also wrote radio commercials and newspapers ads, and even coined a new slogan for the campaign: "Leadership for a Change." And like a dummy I did it all for free.

Why was I doing all this work? Two reasons I guess. The first was ego. After each letter, Mark Kihn would call me up and pour praise all over me. "You are a hero over here," he would exclaim. And Tom Flanagan even wrote me a nice note saying, "I just want to let you know how grateful I am for your help with the Harper campaign's direct mail. Your mastery of the genre is giving us a huge advantage. If we win … you will have had a lot to do with it."

The other reason I helped Stephen was probably more of a rationalization. I had convinced myself that by helping Stephen I was also helping to promote the NCC's agenda and by extension conservative ideology. After all, Stephen's avowed aim was to restore the Canadian Alliance to its conservative roots. That meant he would use his position as Opposition Leader (I never really believed he would ever be elected Prime Minister) to denounce gag laws and call for lower taxes and push for smaller government and all those other wonderful things.

That's why I helped Stephen in other ways, too. In December 2001, for instance, I got a call from Arthur

Finkelstein, the NCC's former political consultant. He told me the Day team was interested in hiring him for their campaign, and that he was seriously considering the offer. But first he wanted my opinion as to whether or not he should take the job. I realized a seasoned political pro like Arthur – who had helped Senators, Governors and Presidents win elections – would make mincemeat out of Harper and his untested campaign team composed of professors and well-meaning amateurs. So, as a favour to me, I asked Arthur to turn down the Day offer, which he did. That act alone probably saved the Harper team's bacon. When I related this episode to Stephen he was suitably grateful for my intervention but also angry, angry at Arthur. He considered it a "betrayal" that Arthur was even talking to the Day camp.

Sometimes my support for Stephen was more personal. In January 2002, for instance, my wife and I drove through a winter storm so we could watch Stephen give a speech to a group of Canadian Alliance members in Burlington. It was the first time I had ever seen Stephen in action as a politician. And he did a great job. His speech was well received and he worked the room like a pro. He had always told me he didn't like doing the things politicians had to do, but he knew how to do them. What's more, he looked great. He had lost lots of weight and was a lean, mean political machine. No more Fatboy. I didn't talk to him at that event because after his speech ended he was mobbed by well-wishers. I just quietly slipped out. I wasn't even sure he had seen me. But after I arrived home I got a phone call. It was Stephen. He just wanted to thank me for showing up. It was the first time he sounded more like a friend than a boss.

From time to time, I also offered Stephen tactical advice, like the time he called me to talk about his relationship with the Christian Right. This had become an issue, because in February 2002, Flanagan had publicly bashed Day's Christian supporters. Flanagan claimed Day was relying too heavily on Pentecostals, anti-abortion Catholics, Orthodox Jews and members of the Dutch Reformed Church for support. He further suggested to the media that Day was trying to string together a coalition of single-interest groups to win. "It is very dangerous for the party if it gets taken over by special interest groups,"[27] declared Flanagan.

Stephen asked me about this antagonistic approach and I told him it was bad strategy. Rather than antagonizing social conservatives and driving them away, I said he needed to treat them with respect because there were plenty of so-cons who were also fiscal conservatives and they could be won over to his side. Stephen agreed with me.

I should also note here, that despite the media portrayal of him as an evangelical bible-thumper, Stephen is actually a social moderate. He regarded social conservatism as a political dead end. "Social conservatives just don't seem to realize they are culturally isolated," was how he put it to me once. "The world has passed them by." During all his time at the NCC, he rarely discussed religion. I don't even know what his religion is, other than that he is some sort of Protestant.

At any rate, when Stephen won the leadership in March 2002, it was one of the most exciting days of my life. I was actually kind of awestruck as I watched Stephen make his acceptance speech on TV. Here was a guy I had worked with so closely, now leading the Canadian Alliance. But the reality of it all really hit me the next morning when, while walking to work, I saw Stephen's face staring at me from every newsstand on the sidewalk. He was now a big-time political player.

The next day, NCC Chairman Colin Brown Jr. sent out the following statement:

"It's a proud day for all the NCC's 40,000 supporters. Stephen's convincing victory ensures that all Canadians who believe in the NCC's values of more freedom and less government will now have a champion in Ottawa. Stephen is a brilliant political thinker, but he's also a principled conservative who as NCC president had the courage to fight for what he believed in. He will now be taking that fight to a larger stage. We wish him well."

As for me, I knew that things were never going to be the same for me or for the NCC.

Mind you, some things did stay the same. Mark Kihn, for instance, still wanted me to write fundraising letters and ad copy. This time, however, he wanted me to do it not for Stephen, but for the Alliance. For me that was going too far. It was one thing to help out Stephen, quite another to work for the party.

Besides, I was starting to feel guilty about my role in Stephen's leadership race. Every dollar I raised for Stephen was one less dollar for the NCC. Every second I worked on Stephen's stuff was one less second I worked on NCC stuff. I was clearly in a conflict of interest.

So I called up Mark to tell him I was quitting: No more work for Stephen, no more work for the Alliance. Mark was not happy about my decision and he tried to lay a guilt trip on me about how Stephen "needed me." I was unmoved. After all, as I told Mark, Stephen now had the resources of the Alliance at his disposal.

It was from that point on that my relationship with Harper's inner circle became somewhat frosty. Not that it mattered. Even though I still supported Stephen and what he was trying to do, I was also determined to make the NCC my only priority. As I was to find out later, that was easier said than done.

CHAPTER 9
TAKING A STAND

MARK KIHN LEFT THE NCC IN MID-2003 TO WORK full-time for the Canadian Alliance, by which time I had become the NCC's main spokesman. As such, I faced a unique dilemma: what do you do when an ex-NCC president is a key political player? Do you treat him like any other politician – praise him when he does something right and criticize him when he does something wrong? Or do you cut him some slack if he compromises his principles because he is our guy.

Initially, I didn't think this would be a problem. I had every confidence Stephen Harper the politician would not be much different from Stephen Harper the NCC president. That is, he would be a true-blue conservative leader. Stephen, after all, wasn't like other politicians. He actually believed in conservatism. But, more than that, he also believed Canada needed a true conservative party. As he once wrote in the NCC newsletter *Freedom Watch*, "Canadians need and deserve more than just strategic alliances. They need an alternative grounded in conservative ideals such as smaller government, lower taxes, the equality of citizens, and the rule of law. For if all we want is the exercise of power, we might as well join the Liberals."[28]

Indeed, the only reason he ran for the leadership of the Canadian Alliance was to ensure Canada did have such a conservative alternative. For all of these reasons, I believed Stephen was going to be a leader who stuck by his values. And I still believed that after he became leader of the Conservative Party in March 2004.

But not long after he became Tory leader, Stephen disappointed me on an issue near and dear to the NCC's heart – Chrétien's election gag law. If anyone knew the dangers of this gag law, Stephen did. One of his last acts as NCC president, after all, was to challenge the Chrétien gag law in the courts.

And, of course, after he left us we continued waging that legal battle, initially with success. In December 2001, the Alberta Court of Queen's Bench ruled parts of Chrétien's gag law to be unconstitutional. A year later, the Alberta Court of Appeal ruled the entire gag law unconstitutional. So far, so good.

Then the case went before the Supreme Court of Canada where, unfortunately, our winning streak came to a screeching halt. On May 17th, 2004, the Supreme Court ruled 6-3 in favour of the gag law. Writing for the majority, Mr. Justice Michel Bastarache declared, "In the absence of spending limits, it is possible for the affluent or a number of persons pooling their resources and acting in concert to dominate the political discourse, depriving their opponents of a reasonable opportunity to speak and be heard, and undermining the voter's ability to be adequately informed of all views."

It was a horrible ruling. The court had essentially killed free election speech in this country. After the ruling came down I faced a media scrum in the court's foyer. "I feel like there's been a death in the family," I said. "This is a devastating ruling. It's bad for democracy; it's bad for freedom; it's bad for Canada." I was truly devastated. Never in my life had I been so disappointed. For 20 years, the NCC had fought to save free political speech and now the fight was over. And we lost.

But at least I could console myself with the knowledge that the NCC now had a political ally in Stephen Harper. Surely he would loudly denounce the Supreme Court ruling and publically pledge to scrap the gag law if elected Prime Minister.

But that didn't happen.

Stephen refused to make any comment on the court's ruling. I couldn't believe it. What the heck was going on? Incensed, I called John McLaughlin, our American consultant, and told him I was going to send out a news release reminding the media that during the 2004 Conservative leadership campaign, Stephen had signed a Free Speech Protection Pledge which declared, "I, Stephen Harper, pledge if elected Prime Minister to protect the democratic freedom of all Canadians by immediately repealing those sections of the Canada Elections Act (commonly known as the election gag law) which deny all Canadians the opportunity to freely and effectively participate in the democratic process."

I knew all about that pledge because it was my idea. I wrote it and I presented it to all the three Tory leadership candidates. (The other two candidates, Tony Clement and Belinda Stronach, signed it as well.)

John calmed me down and convinced me not to say or do anything rash. So I didn't say a word. But I was not happy.

Ironically, not long after the Supreme Court ruling, a federal election was called and I found myself not attacking Stephen but defending him. The media were looking for dirt and they were hoping I could provide it. The CBC, for instance, called me up to ask if Stephen was the kind of boss who "didn't suffer fools gladly?" "Did he have a temper?" "Was he hard to work for?" – that kind of stuff. I knew what they wanted. They wanted me to say something like, "Stephen was an ogre who made us all cry because of his ferocious temper." But I didn't oblige. I simply told them Stephen was a tough boss, but a fair one.

More problematic were the media calls asking about the NCC's stand on healthcare. The NCC and healthcare had become something of an issue in the election, thanks to the Liberals. Just days before the election was called, they issued a report on the NCC which asserted we had one overriding goal: to privatize the healthcare system. It was all part of the Liberal plan to demonize Stephen. When I got calls asking me about this, I knew I had to be careful. The last thing I wanted was a headline in the *Globe and Mail* reading, "Harper will gut medicare, gloats former NCC colleague." So I just told the media the truth. I told them the NCC had lots of other issues on its agenda besides healthcare and that our goal was simply to inject more choice into the system, not gut it. That was just boring enough to satisfy the media, without embarrassing Stephen.

The 2004 election was also the first-ever Canadian election where a gag law was in place. For the first time in the NCC's history we faced legal restrictions on how much money we could spend during a federal election to get out our message. Also, for the first time in our history, we had to register with Elections Canada before we could issue a single political ad. I found the situation quite distasteful. Rather than give in to the gag law, I wanted to fight it, to test it, to see if I could get around it somehow. And I came up with a pretty clever strategy, if I do say so myself.

My plan was to take advantage of the fact that Canadians don't usually distinguish between a provincial party and its federal counterpart. Essentially, they see provincial Liberals and Conservatives as being identical to federal Liberals and Conservatives. This was important because, on the eve of the federal election, Ontario Liberal Premier Dalton McGuinty had unveiled a budget that included the biggest tax hike to hit Ontarians in 11 years. This shocked and angered a lot of Ontarians because by increasing taxes, McGuinty had shattered a key Liberal election promise. McGuinty had even signed a special pledge during the election not to raise taxes without the consent of taxpayers in a referendum.

I saw the voter anger at McGuinty as an opportunity to bash the federal Liberals without breaking the gag law. I quickly put together a newspaper ad with this headline: "Had it with Dalton's Broken Promises ... Then Send the Liberals a Message." And the ad copy included this call to action: "Let them know you have had it with Liberal broken promises; that you have had it with Liberal tax grabs; that you have had it with Liberals and their scandalous contempt for taxpayers. Let them know you're angry. Let them know you're tired of Liberal broken promises."

Now, nowhere in this ad did I mention Liberal Prime Minister Paul Martin or the federal Liberal Party. It was clearly an ad about provincial politics. So technically, it did not qualify as federal election advertising, meaning I could spend as much money as I pleased without fear of infringing the gag law and having RCMP officers storm our office. Nor did I have to register with Elections Canada.

Of course, I couldn't help it if some Ontario voters, after reading our ad, decided to send the Ontario Liberals a message by voting against the federal Liberals. In fact, I was kind of hoping that would happen.

Mind you, everybody knew what I was up to. The CBC's Susan Bonner, for instance, called me up the day the ad appeared in the paper. "Aren't you trying to get around the gag law with this ad?" she asked. Naturally, I was all innocence in my reply. "I don't know what you mean, Susan. This ad is just about Premier McGuinty breaking an election promise. It has nothing to do with the federal election."

I don't think she believed me.

The ad also caused quite a stir among the federal Liberals. I watched with great glee as my old friend Sheila Copps angrily brandished our ad on national television, denouncing us for finding a gag law loophole. And Tim Murphy, from the Prime Minister's Office, got all bent out of shape, too. He claimed on a TV news program that the NCC's ad might actually have violated the gag law. I responded by sending out a news release demanding Murphy apologize. I also used the release to once again attack both the Liberals and the gag law. Here's what I wrote:

"Mr. Murphy hinted on a CTV news program that an NCC newspaper ad which condemned Premier McGuinty for breaking his promises and raising taxes, somehow violated the federal election gag law. Are Murphy and the Liberals actually saying the federal election gag law makes it a crime to comment on provincial issues? Maybe Mr. Murphy doesn't think Ontario voters are smart enough to distinguish between the federal and provincial Liberals. Mr. Murphy's comments should frighten anyone who cares about freedom and democracy. Clearly it seems the

Liberals believe the gag law should be used to stifle all political speech. This law could be even more dangerous than we thought."

We didn't run the McGuinty ad again during the 2004 election. The NCC executive was getting jittery that perhaps Elections Canada would indeed charge us with breaking the gag law. The last thing we needed at that time was more legal bills. And that was OK with me because I had already accomplished what I set out to do. Despite the gag law, I had found a way to get speak out freely and had generated tons of free publicity for the NCC, to boot.

When Stephen lost the 2004 election, we at the NCC were all pretty disappointed for our friend, especially since, in light of the Adscam Scandal, he had a good chance to win. In my view, Stephen lost that election for one simple reason: instead of defining himself, he had allowed the Liberals to define him. In the last few weeks of that campaign, the Liberals unleashed a series of vicious TV ads which portrayed Stephen as a war-mongering, woman-hating, gun-loving clone of Satan.

How did the Tories respond? They ran soft and fuzzy TV ads featuring Stephen playing with his kids. Bad move. They were taking a knife to a gun fight. If Stephen was going to win the next election, I reasoned, he would need people around him who knew how to run a more media-savvy campaign. He would need a tough guy. That's why I tried to arrange a meeting between Stephen and Arthur Finkelstein. But nothing ever came of it. And that's too bad, because Arthur could have shown Stephen how to win an election while keeping a conservative message.

Unfortunately, Stephen wasn't getting that kind of advice. After the 2004 election, the Conservative Party opted to play down Stephen's ideology, preferring instead to present him to the Canadian public as some sort of likeable guy.

During the summer of 2004, for instance, Stephen embarked on a cross-country barbecue tour to show off his friendliness. When a reporter from the *National Post* asked me about this strategy I was honest, "From my perspective I think they are making a mistake," I said. "Instead of trying to get people to like Stephen they should be working on getting people to agree with him." By that I meant they should be focusing on selling Stephen's vision, not his personality.

I thought it was an innocuous enough comment, really just free advice. But some people in the Conservative Party didn't take kindly to it. A couple of days after my comments appeared in print, we received a nasty little letter from a Dr. Ian Brodie, an academic who served as one of Stephen's inner circle. He wasn't happy. Brodie complained my comments were not helping the party. As soon as I read that letter, I fully understood Stephen's problem. It seemed to me he had surrounded himself with egghead amateurs who clearly didn't have a clue as to what they were doing.

Rather than writing petulant letters, Brodie should have welcomed criticism from the right. After all, Conservatives needed pressure from the right to offset those pushing them from the left. Stephen Harper once understood this. While still a Reform MP, he told an NCC gathering, "The Reform Party needs people who will support us when we are right and we need people who will be willing to oppose us when we are wrong."[29] Former Ontario Premier Mike Harris understood this too. While speaking at an NCC event, Harris said he expected and hoped the NCC would take him to task should his party ever stray from its ideological roots.

But then again, Harris actually wanted to implement a conservative agenda. And the more I watched the Tory party evolve in late 2004, the more worried I became that the party was losing its way. Simply put, the Tories were doing very little to set themselves apart from the Liberals on issues like taxes, government spending and healthcare.

So Brodie or no Brodie, I decided to take action to push the Conservatives in the right direction. The place to do it, I figured, was at the Conservative Party convention of March, 2005.

To do the job, I put together a multi-pronged PR strategy. A couple of days before the convention started, I had an op-ed in the *National Post* urging Tory delegates to come up with a truly conservative agenda, an agenda that challenged Liberalism instead of aping it. "Why would anybody vote for Liberal-Lite," I wrote, "when they can get the real deal? ... When Conservatives dabble with left-wing policies they end up alienating conservative Canada – the people who actually support the party and the people who need to be encouraged to show up on election day." Then I concluded by saying, "I offer this advice, not so much for the sake of the Conservative Party, but for the sake of democracy. After all, having to choose between a Liberal party and a Liberal party wannabe doesn't give voters much of a choice."[30]

Then when the convention was underway, I placed a full-page newspaper ad in the *National Post*, warning the party not to "take a left turn." And as a final little bit of political guerrilla warfare, I and other NCC staff members handed out hundreds of "No Left Turn" buttons on the convention floor. But I was fighting a losing cause.

The overall tone of the convention reflected a Conservative Party that wished to downplay ideology. Several Reform-style policies were dropped from the party platform. Virtually no speaker at the conference talked about reducing the size of government or promoting free markets or protecting individual freedoms. It was all just about beating the Liberals.

Yet, when Stephen won a minority government in January 2006, I couldn't help but feel excited. And why not? My old boss, my friend, the ex-president of the NCC, was now the Prime Minister of Canada. It was an amazing day in the history of our organization. I wondered at the time what Colin Brown Sr. would have thought about such a turn of events. I was also hopeful, thinking that perhaps now, with a successful election behind him, Stephen would return to his old NCC form and govern Canada like a true conservative. As I wrote in an op-ed at the time, "Canadians are ready to turn the page and to set a new course. They want, in short, the government they deserve at a price they can afford. It's time for politicians to heed the voters. It's time to give Canadians a government they can be proud of again."[31]

It didn't take long for my optimistic bubble to burst. In fact, on the very day Stephen was sworn in as Prime Minister, he accepted both a floor crossing Liberal MP (David Emerson) and an unelected Senator into his cabinet. Not a good sign. Nor was it a good sign when just prior to the swearing-in ceremony, Ian Brodie, who was to become Stephen's Chief of Staff, cornered our chairman, who was attending the event as the NCC's representative, so he could personally berate me. It seems Brodie took strong exception to my "no left turn" antics at the Tory convention.

Things didn't get much better after that. In his first year as Prime Minister, Stephen offered little in the way of conservative leadership. In fact, some of the steps he took seemed directly opposed to what he stood for while he was NCC president. For instance, he didn't scrap, or even move to loosen, the election gag law. Nor did he move to scrap the election blackout law. Those two omissions were disappointing enough. But what's worse was that he actually imposed his own version of a gag law. I am talking about the Conservative government's Federal Accountability Act, which included a measure making it illegal for individuals to contribute more than $1,100 per year to a candidate or political party. This was done, say the Conservatives, to "eliminate once and for all the influence of rich, wealthy individuals from the political process."

Hearing that kind of language coming from the Conservative Party made me quite uncomfortable. It reminded me of the way the Liberals used to talk when they infringed on free speech with election gag laws. And make no mistake, the Conservative limit on political contributions – like the Liberal election gag law – infringes on free speech. Think about it. When I make a contribution to a political party I am making a political statement. For the state to limit my right to donate my own money to my own political cause is to limit my democratic right of expression.

I had another concern with the Tory contribution limit. Once politicians start limiting how much citizens can contribute to political parties, it won't be long before they – in the interest of creating a level playing field– start to impose limits on how much money citizens can contribute to independent advocacy groups like the NCC.

Stephen used to understand these dangers when he was with the NCC. So why, I wondered, had he done an about-face? Why was he suddenly in favour of restricting free expression? Why wasn't he taking any actions to scrap Canada's election gag laws? Could it be that he now supported gag laws?

145

It's also possible that Stephen imposed the contribution limit as a way of hampering the Liberal Party's ability to raise money. Unlike the Conservatives, who have a wide network of grassroots support, the Liberals traditionally rely on fewer and wealthier donors, so a tight contribution limit puts them at a definite fundraising disadvantage. Yes, putting the Liberals in such a bind might be smart politics. But it's also morally wrong. The Conservatives should not be using their power to undermine their political opponents. To do so is to allow cynical, political pragmatism to trump principle.

And it's not just about the Liberals. Contribution limits will also make it exceedingly difficult for new parties to emerge. Typically newer parties lack the infrastructure and expertise needed to raise small donations from large groups of people. To get started they would, out of necessity, require a few large donations. But the contribution limits make that virtually impossible.

For all of these reasons, I was not happy with the direction Stephen was taking on this important issue. It seemed to me he was hindering democracy, not helping it.

I was also surprised at how Stephen openly pandered to Quebec nationalists. Short of wearing a Montreal Canadiens jersey in the House of Commons, he was doing everything possible to woo the Quebec nationalist vote. His biggest move in that direction came in November 2006 when he introduced a resolution in the House of Commons declaring "the Québécois form a nation within a united Canada." This, to say the least, was unStephen-like. Back in his NCC days, he always opposed the idea of cozying up to Quebec nationalists.

In fact, if anything, he liked to rattle their cage. As I noted earlier, as NCC president he had subsidized Brent Tyler's court battles against Quebec's anti-English language laws. And he had vehemently opposed granting Quebec any sort of special status. He believed all Canadians should be treated equally no matter where they lived in Canada. In fact, the very first NCC campaign he directed was our opposition in 1997 to the Calgary Declaration.

Signed by all provincial premiers (except Quebec's), the Calgary Declaration stated, "In Canada's federal system, where respect for diversity and equality underlies unity, the unique character of Quebec society, including its French-speaking majority, its culture, and its tradition of civil law, is fundamental to the well being of Canada. Consequently, the legislature and government of Quebec have a role to protect and develop the unique character of Quebec society within Canada."

Stephen called this Declaration nothing but an "appeasement" of ethnic nationalism. He wanted to fight it. Under his guidance, the NCC sought to undermine public support for the Declaration with a series of newspaper ads declaring that "unique" was the same as "distinct." This was, of course, a reference to the failed and unpopular Meech Lake and Charlottetown Accords which would have recognized Quebec as a "distinct society."

Yet now that he was Prime Minister, Stephen was grandly declaring the Québécois a nation. It certainly seemed as if he were playing the same kind of tribal politics he once so thoroughly abhorred.

Then there was his surprise move, in late 1996, to impose a tax on income trusts. Now, I am not an economist or an accountant, and to be frank, I never really understood the ins and outs of the income trust issue. But I did know one thing: Stephen had made a solemn election pledge not to impose such a tax. In fact, here's what Stephen wrote in the *National Post* a year earlier: "The government claims that income trusts enjoy an unfair tax advantage over corporate dividends. If they believe this, then the answer is not to shut down a valuable investment vehicle, but to cut the double taxation of dividends. In short, level the playing field and let the market decide between income trusts and dividend-paying companies."[32]

As NCC president, Stephen had always made a big deal about political accountability and politicians keeping their promises. He had even helped people sue the BC government for allegedly lying about an election promise. And yet, now, here he was breaking a promise.

I was also taken aback at the Conservative government's defence of the new tax. Finance Minister Jim Flaherty justified the move with weak left-wing sounding arguments that could have come straight out of the NDP or Liberal playbooks. Here are a couple of Flaherty quotes to illustrate my point:

- "After all, someone has to pay the taxes for healthcare and education, all the good things we love as Canadians."

- "If corporations don't pay their fair share of taxes, this tax burden will shift ... This is simply not fair."

What? I thought the Tories were supposed to be about making taxes lower, not fairer.

There's one other thing I understood about the income trust issue – the Prime Minister's tax was making NCC supporters very angry. Our office was flooded with phone calls and emails from irate NCC supporters who wanted us to demand the Prime Minister keep his word. We were also getting lots of calls from people who were not NCC supporters, urging us to do the same thing.

So what did we do? In a word, nothing. Rather than launching an NCC-style broadside against the Prime Minister for breaking an election pledge, we simply ran a tepid newspaper ad urging the government to increase the phase-in period for the new tax from four to ten years. Likewise the NCC did nothing to oppose the limits imposed on political contributions. We did nothing to urge Stephen to scrap the election gag law. And we did nothing to oppose his resolution recognizing the Québécois as a nation.

Why the kid gloves treatment? Simple. I still wanted to give Stephen the benefit of the doubt. I still hoped the "real" Stephen Harper would yet emerge.

However, by early 2007, I could no longer hold my fire. By then I had come to realize Prime Minister Stephen Harper was not the same man as NCC president Stephen Harper. My epiphany came when the Harper government went on a massive pre-budget spending spree, dishing out a whopping $12 billion in just three months. And a large portion of the spending was targeted to those provinces where the Tories hoped to make voting gains: Quebec and Ontario.

This was the kind of cynical spending game the Liberals liked to play. And had it been the Liberals engaging in that kind of reckless spending, I would have bashed them for it. I knew that for the sake of the NCC's credibility I now had to bash the Conservatives. The time had come for me to speak out against my old boss.

So I wrote an op-ed in the *Globe and Mail*, which stated, "Even the most ardent Harper apologist would have to concede these spending announcements ... are more about helping the Conservatives win the next election than about a wise of use tax dollars."[33] I repeated those comments on radio and on national TV.

Little did I know that worse was yet to come.

In March 2007, Finance Minister Jim Flaherty unveiled a budget which, to be blunt, was a disaster. It was an orgy of massive government spending. As columnist Andrew Coyne wrote, "The $200-billion in program spending Mr.

Flaherty has budgeted for this year works out to about $5,800 for every man, woman and child in Canada. Even adjusting for inflation and increases in population, that's more than Paul Martin spent in his frantic last hours. It is more than the Mulroney government spent in its last days. It is more than the Trudeau government spent in the depths of the early 1980s recession. All of these past benchmarks of out-of-control spending must now be retired. Jim Flaherty has outdone them all."[34]

And just as bad, despite having a $13 billion surplus, the budget contained no broad-based tax cuts. As Jason Clemons and Niels Veldhuis of the Fraser Institute put it, "The federal budget … was conservative in name only."[35]

That budget, combined with the pre-budget spending splurge, was the last straw. After that, I knew Stephen had no intention of providing Canadians with conservative government, or of even paying lip service to conservative ideals. He had turned his back on conservatism. Consequently, as far as I was concerned, there was no more giving Stephen the benefit of the doubt. I was going to treat him like any other cynical, free-spending politician.

I first vented my frustration on my blog where I wrote, "Somebody remind me again, who is running the federal government, Conservatives or Liberals? I have to ask because today's budget sure looks like something the Liberals or maybe even the NDP could have concocted."

I also denounced the budget in a news release and on national TV and radio. I wrote a scathing op-ed which

151

appeared in the Sun News Media chain, in which I wrote, "The Tory budget is bad for taxpayers, it's bad for our economy and it's ultimately bad for the Conservative Party. It seems Jim Flaherty has forgotten the words of former U.S. president Ronald Reagan who said, 'The problem is not that people are taxed too little, the problem is that government spends too much'."[36]

And for good measure, I sent a letter to the editor which appeared in the *National Post,* complaining about Stephen's generosity to Quebec just prior to that province's provincial election. "Our Prime Minister poured about $3-billion into la belle province," I wrote. "If this was done to help the Jean Charest-led Liberals defeat the separatists, it worked. Mr. Charest ended up winning a minority government of 48 seats, which works out to about $63-million per seat. Good thing Mr. Harper wasn't paying for a Liberal majority – that might have bankrupted the country."[37]

I knew full well that taking such an outspoken stance would likely anger Stephen and his minions in the Prime Minister's Office. But I didn't care. I figured it was time I started doing my job. And my job wasn't to make friends in high places. It was to provide a voice for Canadians who wanted less government and more freedom.

Besides, it had always been an NCC tradition to go after Conservative politicians who turned their back on conservative principles. Back in the days when David Somerville led the NCC, we were quite blunt in our attacks on Prime Minister Brian Mulroney for his failure to cut government spending, and for his decision to impose the GST. And during his time at the NCC, Stephen had openly criticized Preston Manning, Stockwell Day and Mike Harris when they failed to live up to his standards.

What's more, in 2002, I had not been shy about criticizing then Ontario Premier Ernie Eves for abandoning conservative principles. In fact, not only did I criticize Eves, but I sent out a mass mailing to NCC supporters in Ontario, urging them to defer their financial support to the Ontario PC Party.

As I noted in a news release: "We want our supporters, many of whom also support the Ontario PCs, to let Premier Ernie Eves know that they don't want him to backtrack on the promises of the Common Sense Revolution. And the best way for them to get that message out is to hit the Tory Party where it hurts the most – in the pocketbook."

My purpose was to give the Ontario Tories a political wake-up call.

As I put it then, "If Eves thinks he can win the next election by scrapping the principles and abandoning his political base, he's mistaken. Conservatives in Ontario won't be taken for granted. They will make their voices heard."

In 2007, I was prepared to take the same sort of action against the Harper Tories, to give them a political wake-up call, to keep nagging Stephen with news releases and op-eds and ad campaigns, until he started doing the right thing. At least that was my plan.

But then on the morning of April 4th, NCC president Peter Coleman called me into our boardroom. Peter, an accountant who had been the NCC's Treasurer for years, had taken on the duties of NCC president in 2006. He was the most laid back president the NCC ever had. And he was generous, too. He had okayed the NCC buying me a cell phone and a laptop computer, which Stephen (the cheapskate) had refused to do.

But on that morning, Peter wasn't looking laid back or generous. He looked grim. I sat across from him at the conference board table. "What's up?" I asked. He averted his eyes and said, "Gerry, we have decided to take a different direction. Your employment is terminated, effective immediately."

What? I was stunned, shocked. All I could utter was, "But why?" He slid a brown envelope to me. "I am not going into that. Here's your severance package."

Then he silently slunk out of the room. I sat there in a state of shock until a representative from an employment agency suddenly popped into the room and escorted me out of the building. I was not even allowed to go back to my office or say goodbye to my fellow staff members. Just like that, my 22-year career with the NCC was over.

When I got home, still dazed, instinct and training took over. I sent out an email to all my media contacts telling them I was no longer employed with the NCC. Then the calls and emails started pouring in from the *Globe and Mail*, from *the National Post*, from the *Toronto Star*, from CTV and CBC. "Why were you fired?" they all asked. "Were you fired as punishment for criticizing Stephen Harper?"

It was a question I didn't know how to answer.

NCC PRESIDENT PETER COLEMAN WAS ADAMANT that my termination had nothing to do with my outspoken criticism of Stephen. As he said to the *Toronto Star*, "We would never muzzle anybody and if anybody in the Conservative party called me and told me to not say something, I'd tell them to get lost."[38] Then a day after my firing, on the NCC's website, somebody from the office wrote: "All of the media interviews yesterday asked if there was any political pressure on us as we had recently been critical of the spending that was made in the last federal budget. We reminded the media that we take our cue from our members and not the PMO."[39] So that was the official word. My criticism of Stephen Harper had nothing to do with my firing.

So why was I let go? Well, maybe Peter simply believed I was incompetent. That's a good theory, except for one thing. A few months earlier at my performance review, Peter actually praised my work and even gave me a discretionary cash bonus. So clearly, at that time at least, he must have thought I was doing a good job. Nor did I have any inkling NCC members wanted me fired. After my firing I was flooded with phone calls and emails from long-time NCC supporters who expressed shock and dismay at my termination. Many of them still keep in regular contact with me. So the bottom line is, I can't say for certain why I was fired. Nobody at the NCC ever gave me an explanation.

But while the true reason for my firing remains a mystery, one thing is clear – the NCC has definitely changed its tone since my departure.

Just consider the first NCC newsletter to come out after my termination. It had a completely different take on the 2007 federal budget than mine. Whereas I had blasted that budget as a big spending, Liberal-style monstrosity, the now Nicholls-less NCC described it this way: "This is a budget designed to appeal to voters in suburban Canada, gaining the Tories favour in areas like the vote rich GTA and rural Quebec. Pensioners and families with young children are the winners in this budget. To these groups … the mix of targeted tax cuts and social spending will probably come as a welcome surprise … All in all this was a 'minority' budget and while it focused far too heavily on spending, we can only hope that it will firm up enough support to form a majority government."[40]

And during the 2008 federal election campaign, the NCC's official blog offered what seemed like an endorsement of the Conservative party with this statement:

"Except for the Conservative party, all our federal parties have proposed to significantly increase spending, increase taxes or increase both ... So before you bombard me with e-mails accusing me of being bias*(sic)* towards the Conservative party – get over it! The fact is the Conservatives are the only party talking about keeping federal spending under control. I do not have to wait and see the Conservative platform to know that it will contain only a fraction of the spending the other four parties have initiated."[41]

It's impossible to imagine former NCC presidents Colin Brown Sr. or David Somerville endorsing a Conservative platform in such a manner. They would at least wait to read it first. But then again, David and Colin Sr. fervently believed the NCC should be about promoting ideas, not partisan politics. But now the NCC appears to be hoping for a Conservative majority government and using language to praise the Tories that could have been lifted from the party's official talking points.

In fact, that's the role I believe Stephen Harper wants the conservative movement to play. Not content with running the Conservative party, he also wants to run the conservative movement, to transform it into a compliant cheerleader for his policies.

That's something I will always resist.

Indeed, if anybody thought losing my job would

intimidate me into silence, they must have been gravely disappointed. Not long after I became independent (which sounds much better than unemployed), I launched what the *Calgary Herald*'s Nigel Hannaford called a "one-man guerrilla war on the Conservatives' right flank."[42] Through op-eds in national newspapers, through appearances on TV and radio programs, through countless interviews with journalists and through organized public debates, I relentlessly condemned the Harper government's abandonment of conservative principles. In a sense, like Colin Brown Sr. in the 1960s, I had become a one-man band for freedom. And in the process I also became the media's "go to guy" on conservatism. Whenever a reporter or producer wanted a true conservative perspective on the Harper government, they called me.

Why did I take on this role? After all, it would have been a lot easier for me to see the errors of my ways and seek the Tory government's forgiveness, in the hopes of landing a plum patronage appointment somewhere. But that's just not me. I had spent nearly half my life fighting for freedom and I was not about to change now. Plus, I realized my firing was sending a message to other conservative activists. As the *Globe and Mail* reported, "Mr. Nicholls's departure has sparked nervousness in some other non-governmental and conservative-leaning groups. The leaders of one such group, who asked to remain unidentified, expressed concern that Mr. Nicholls's exit might chill some organizations from speaking out."[43] I did not want Stephen to think he could bully the conservative movement into submission. And, indeed, since starting my crusade I have been approached by countless conservatives who, like me, are disillusioned with the Harper Tories.

But I had another reason to stand strong. I wanted to make amends for my earlier weakness. During my time at the NCC, I had allowed myself to get caught up in Stephen's political career. In so doing, I had turned my back on the NCC's basic principle of non-partisanship. Did I not help Stephen in his Canadian Alliance leadership campaign? Did I not pull my punches when he first showed signs of abandoning NCC principles? Did I not allow my own ego to obscure my values? I had let down the conservative movement. I had let down NCC supporters. Most of all, I had let down the legacy of Colin Brown Sr. That will never happen again.

Not that I ever expected my lone voice could push the Conservative Party in the right direction. How could it? The Conservative Party these days is dominated by what I like to call power people, people who care only about holding power for the sake of holding power. These are people who view conservative ideology as a dead weight, something that must be chucked over the side if the party is ever going to ascend to the heavens of majority government power.

The main proponent of this view is Tom Flanagan, Stephen's one-time Chief of Staff. An intellectual, Flanagan likes to see politics in terms of theories. In his book *Harper's Team*, for instance, he talks about the "median voter theorem," which he defines thusly: "It shows mathematically ...

parties will converge on the position of the median voter. A party that stations itself away from the midpoint yields more than half the potential voters to the other party and thus will lose the election."[44]

In other words, Flanagan argues the Tories must adopt policy platforms that appeal to the greatest mass of voters possible. And since according to Flanagan, conservatism doesn't appeal to a great mass of voters, it must be dropped. "Canada is not yet a conservative or Conservative country," he wrote. "We can't win votes if we veer too far to the right of the median voter."[45] So rather than pushing ideology, the Tories have adopted a strategy called incrementalism, meaning they will only introduce conservatism in tiny incremental steps.

In the name of incrementalism, Stephen hasn't cut government spending, he has increased it. He hasn't made government smaller, he has made it bigger. He hasn't got government out of the economy, but has taken to meddling in the free market by introducing burdensome regulations. Rather than treating all citizens equally, he has blatantly pandered to Quebec nationalists.

Of course, other conservative leaders – Margaret Thatcher, Ronald Reagan, Mike Harris – have not always lived up to their principles while in power. But at least they always talked like conservatives and promoted conservatism. Not Stephen. He has never used his office to extol free markets or individual freedom or less government. Instead, he praises our socialist healthcare system, complains about capitalists "who care more about the almighty dollar than the safety of their customers[46]" and embraces the global warming gospel of Al Gore. (Stephen's move to ban incandescent light bulbs was nanny-statism at its worst.)

In short, incrementalism seems to require that Stephen not even be perceived as a conservative. This was evident during the 2008 federal election leadership debate. All the other party leaders at the table kept trying to convince Stephen he was a conservative. He kept reassuring them he wasn't. To incrementalists, conservatism is an embarrassment.

Even worse is that the ideology-less Conservatives have also transformed their party into something of a personality cult, centered on Stephen Harper. As Andrew Coyne put it, Harper "has made the Conservatives into legitimate contenders for power, in short, at the expense of conservatism. In its place he offers ... himself."[47] Canadians are supposed to support Stephen not because of his ideas, but because he is a strong leader and a brilliant strategist.

It is true that since coming to power Stephen has consistently put tactics and strategy ahead of ideology. Even when he implements a measure which might be considered conservative he does so not because it's the right thing to do, but because it confers some sort of political advantage to his party. His cut to the GST falls into this category, as do those various Tory tax cuts which have been targeted to carefully selected voter demographics. And to throw a bone to his old Reform base, otherwise alienated by the

Tory's lack of a conservative agenda, Stephen has pushed a few populist hot buttons, such as taking a tough stance on law and order issues and denying tax credits to films and television shows deemed to be offensive.

But the problem with divorcing tactics and ideology, is that it produces a government that places political expediency ahead of principle. As conservative writer and author Paul Tuns has observed, "Rather than being an extreme right-wing conservative, Harper has cleverly hidden that he is a liberal or, at best, a pragmatist who is willing to buck any principle for short-term political advantage."[48] What this means in practice is that whenever their policies meet with resistance, the first instinct of Conservatives is to retreat.

We saw this quite clearly with the Tory stance on the war in Afghanistan. The Tories initially painted themselves as staunch supporters of our effort to battle terrorism in that country. But as the war became increasingly unpopular (especially in Quebec), the Conservatives flip-flopped and announced they would not commit troops to Afghanistan past 2011. As conservative writer Rondi Adamson lamented, "I found this decision to be enormously disappointing. Foreign policy was one area to which I could always point when conservatives bemoaned Harper's tepid attempts at making Canada grow up."[49]

Of course, a truly principled political party makes decisions based not on what's popular, but on what it considers to be right. As former U.S. president Harry Truman once put it, "How far would Moses have gone if he had taken a poll in Egypt? ... It isn't polls or public opinion of the moment that counts. It's right and wrong and leadership."

And leadership is what the Conservative party is lacking. Instead of providing Canadians with a conservative vision, instead of trying to sell conservative ideas to Canadian voters, instead of being a true leader, Stephen has opted to take the path of least resistance. Like a rudderless ship, he is content to float along with the current of public opinion. And if that means acting and talking and governing like a Liberal, so be it. To paraphrase former British Prime Minister Margaret Thatcher, Stephen is willing to do what is wrong because he is afraid to do what's right.

What's more, Stephen's abandonment of his conservative values seems to have blunted his famed tactical brilliance. The biggest political story of 2008 was a constitutional crisis Stephen triggered with his ill-fated plan to end public subsidies for political parties.

In a year-end economic statement, the Conservatives announced they were going to eliminate the public subsidy political parties currently enjoy. It was a good idea. In fact, when I worked at the NCC, I had opposed this subsidy which allows political parties to rake in millions of tax dollars a year. It's wasteful and undemocratic. Taxpayers should not be forced to subsidize political parties. I called it a "welfare plan for politicians."

Yet, Stephen wanted to eliminate this welfare for politicians scheme not for ideological reasons or to save the taxpayers' money. He simply saw it as a clever way to bankrupt the Liberal Party. Otherwise, he would have coupled his plan to scrap the subsidy with a promise to reform Canada's campaign finance laws, in order to make it easier for the Liberals and other parties to raise money through voluntary contributions. Had he done so, it would have taken some of the sting out of his plan to end the subsidy, and it likely would have passed.

Instead, Stephen the brilliant strategist, the masterful tactician, the grand political chess master, opted to box the Liberals into a corner. Without the subsidy the Liberals would have faced a serious financial crisis. Hence they faced a stark choice: they could either fight or die. And putting your enemy in such a situation is always a bad idea – even a rabbit will fight if it's cornered. A wise strategist always leaves room for his enemy to retreat. As Sun Tzu put it, "Do not thwart an enemy retreating home. If you surround the enemy, leave an outlet; do not press an enemy that is cornered."

Stephen didn't give the Liberals an outlet. Not surprisingly, they fought back, formed a coalition with the other opposition parties and nearly toppled his government. As a result, the Tories went into full retreat mode and abandoned their plans to scrap the subsidy.

As that political crisis was playing out, I wondered if the Tories were even worth defending. What difference does it make who runs the government if both the Liberals and Conservatives would offer the same big government policies. Sadly, the Conservatives, like the Liberals, care about one thing and one thing only: power.

Mind you, jaded warrior that I am, it shouldn't really surprise or sadden me that a political party would place expediency ahead of principle. It's a time-honoured practice. What does surprise and sadden me is that my old comrade, Stephen Harper, would go down that cynical road.

Stephen Harper, after all, was the former president of the NCC. He was as ideologically hard-core conservative as they come. He was a man who explicitly went back into politics to fight for true conservatism. And he took that step because he believed then – as I believe now – that it's possible to win elections by emphasizing conservative ideals. Yet even Stephen could not stay true to his values. What happened? Why did Stephen change?

Those are questions I am asked all the time. And I don't really have good answers. How is it that Stephen Harper, of all people, could succumb to the lure of power? Did he have bad advisors? Maybe, but ever since I knew him, Stephen Harper's chief advisor was always Stephen Harper. So that theory doesn't wash. Is he perhaps waiting to spring a true conservative program on the country should he ever win a majority government – the so-called hidden agenda theory? This is an idea many conservatives want to believe. But it doesn't wash either. Let's face it, if the Tories were to win a majority by moving to the left, it would only encourage them to keep moving to the left. Besides, it's irrelevant. If the Harper Tories could not win a majority government with the hapless Stéphane Dion as their primary opponent, they never will.

Unfortunately, the most likely answer to what happened to Stephen is also the most disturbing. Ultimately he didn't have the courage of his convictions. Rather than fighting for what he truly believed, he opted to cop out. I say that not in anger, but in sorrow. For if Stephen won't provide true conservative political leadership, who will? He was the conservative movement's last best hope. And here's the real heartbreak – I believe if Stephen had stuck by his values he would have won his much coveted majority government and Canada would be a better country today because of it.

But alas, it was not to be. He didn't change the system. The system changed him.

With the benefit of hindsight, I now realize it was a supreme mistake for Stephen to go back into partisan politics. He could have done more to promote conservatism had he stayed at the NCC. After all, as NCC president he didn't have to worry about winning seats in Quebec or keeping Red Tories happy or working in a minority government. With his credibility, his intelligence, and his media savvy, he could have helped to sell conservatism to the Canadian public. In short, instead of focusing on winning elections, Stephen, as NCC president, could have focused on something much more important – winning the war of ideas.

Make no mistake – winning the war of ideas is more

important than winning elections. Why? Well, if conservatives can win this war, if we can win Canadians over to our side, it will create a demand in the political marketplace for small government policies. And when that happens, politicians will seek to meet that demand out of their own self-interest.

Take, for instance, the battle to protect free speech from the politically correct censors who operate Canada's Human Rights Commissions. It's the conservative movement, not the Conservative Party, which is fighting that battle. It's small c conservative activists, people like Ezra Levant and Kathy Shaidle and Connie Fournier, who are courageously mobilizing public opinion on this issue.

The conservative movement must lead so that political parties will follow. Just imagine if we could create a political climate where the biggest policy difference between the Prime Minister and the Leader of the Opposition was who wanted to cut taxes the most. As conservative writer Joseph Ben-Ami put it, by explaining conservative principles to the public and highlighting their benefits, conservatives can "expand the envelope of what's possible for a conservative party to achieve in office, while reducing the scope of what non-conservative parties can impose."[50]

That's exactly what the NCC was trying to accomplish in its golden age. We were not a lobby group. Our goal wasn't to influence legislation or to tell politicians what to do. Our goal was to use the media, and sometimes the courts, to raise public awareness and to educate Canadians as to the value of free markets and individual freedom. We wanted Canadians to lobby politicians. We wanted them to demand our governments do the right thing.

The NCC could only be effective in this important role if it was perceived as non-partisan. And so it must be for the entire conservative movement. As I have learned the hard way, the party and the movement must remain separate and distinct. I say that for two reasons.

First, the minute conservatives offer their unconditional support for the Conservative Party is the minute the Conservative Party will betray conservatives. That sounds harsh, but it's the reality of politics. Once politicians think they own you, they feel it's safe to ignore you. That's exactly why the Harper Tories moved to the left. Believing they had the small c conservative vote safely in their pocket – who else are they going to vote for? – their strategy became about winning Liberals over to their side.

The second problem with offering blind allegiance to the Conservative Party, is that rather than being guardians of ideas, conservatives risk becoming no better than paid party hacks. They end up defending Tory policies even if they may be wrong, and attacking opposition policies even if they may be right. This, needless to say, only serves to corrupt the movement.

Only an independent conservative movement can remain true to its ideals. Only an independent conservative movement can, through good old-fashioned activism, prod political parties of all stripes to spend less, to regulate less and to tax less.

Of course, before the conservative movement can win converts and prod politicians, it must have a strong voice. It needs not only to propagate its ideas through the media, but to rally and mobilize Canadians to take action. Unfortunately, the conservative voice in Canada is too weak. That's not to say we have no voice at all. The Canadian Taxpayers Federation does a good job of tracking government waste. And Canada has numerous think thanks – the Fraser Institute, the CD Howe Institute, the Montreal Economic Institute, the Atlantic Institute for Market Studies, the Frontier Centre for Public Policy Analysis – all of which do an excellent job of making the intellectual case for freedom. There are exciting new idea-oriented groups on the horizon like the Institute for Liberal Studies. But to win the war of ideas, you can't rely solely on intellectual arguments or on studies and research papers.

If my experience at the NCC taught me anything, it's that good ideas are not enough. You have to take those ideas and package them in a way that's interesting and exciting, and you have to use emotion to make your case. You need pigs on billboards. You need to target bad guys. You can't be afraid to rock boats or to be controversial or to wage a little hard-edged political guerrilla warfare to expose big government excess.

To be blunt, Canada needs a national organization with

the resources and know-how to do what the NCC used to do in its prime. We need an organization that will provide a strong, independent, undiluted, principled voice for conservatism.

And one aim of such an organization should be to keep a vigilant eye on conservative parties. This is certainly the role taken on by one of the United States' most successful conservative organizations, The Club for Growth. The Club's goal is to elect Republicans who would shrink government, cut taxes, and liberalize trade. It does this by mounting hard-hitting media campaigns and by supporting pro-freedom candidates with direct financial aid.

Unlike other conservative organizations, the Club does not shrink away from opposing moderate Republicans. In fact, the club invented the RINO (Republican in Name Only) Watch list to monitor "Republican office holders around the nation who have advanced egregious anti-growth, anti-freedom or anti-free market policies." The Club has also helped elect conservative Democrats running against liberal Republicans. "A lot of people who donated to the Club for Growth were Cato Institute and Reason Foundation donors," says Club Founder Steve Moore. "People who were libertarians or conservatives first and Republicans second."[51]While this has created some Club enemies in the Republican establishment, it has not stopped the organization from growing.

Any new conservative group could certainly take advantage

of emerging communication technologies which are making it easier than ever to transmit ideas and mobilize citizens. Certainly with the availability of computers and the Internet, it's a lot easier to communicate today than it was back in the late 1960s, when Colin Brown Sr. used costly full-page newspaper ads to get his ideas across. Now, admittedly, I am a bit of a dinosaur when it comes to this type of technology. In fact, if it weren't for my kids, I wouldn't even be able to turn my computer on.

However, the one thing I do know is that by using e-mail and Facebook and blogs and YouTube, conservatives can reach a lot of people quickly and at very little cost.

Just look at what's happened in the United States, where the value of Internet politicking is already clear. Politicians like Democrat Howard Dean and Republican Ron Paul not only raised millions of dollars through blogs and the Internet, they also created powerful online activist movements. Here in Canada, bloggers like the Blogging Tories and the *Western Standard's* Shotgun Blog are providing conservatives with a strong voice in the blogosphere. And Canadian blogger extraordinaire, Stephen Taylor, has used his blog to help expose left-wing bias in the media, even forcing the CBC to apologize for errors that he brought out into the open.

So we have the tools, we have the ideas, we have the people. It's just a matter of putting it all together.

Can such a principled organization be successful in

today's Canada? To borrow a phrase from Barack Obama, yes it can. There are many principled conservatives and libertarians out there who are disillusioned with the failure of our political leaders to promote a small government agenda. But we need to mobilize them. A political vacuum exists today just like it did in 1967, when Colin Brown Sr. decided to provide a voice for true conservatives with his hobby that went berserk. Someone has to step forward and fill that vacuum today.

If the disappointment of the Harper government has taught us anything, it's that we conservatives can't depend on politicians to fight our battles. It's up to us. Unless the Canadian conservative movement acts quickly to assert itself, the fight for freedom in this country will be lost. We can't allow that to happen.

The time for action is now.

ARTIST'S BANANA DRAINS CASH

"Look up in the sky, it's a bird, it's a plane … no wait, it's a giant banana … from Canada!"

Some befuddled Texan may actually have uttered those words had Montreal artist Cesar Saez been able to turn his dream into reality.

What was Saez's dream?

Well, he wanted to build a 300-metre yellow banana and float it in geostationary orbit above Texas.

Think that's funny?

Well here's something even funnier – you, the Canadian taxpayer, helped to fund this fruity project.

Yes that's right.

Saez received a cool $55,000 from the Canada Council for the Arts, a government agency which has a mandate to support the arts apparently by wasting tax dollars in the most outrageous manner possible

Mind you, the Canada Council grant wasn't nearly enough money to finance the banana project; Seaz, in fact, needed more than $1 million.

Who knew creating a flying banana would be so expensive?

Anyway, to help raise the rest of the cash, Saez turned to private investors.

Unfortunately for him, however, private investors don't share the same sophisticated artistic tastes as the Canada Council; he fell short of his goal by about $1 million.

Big surprise.

And so a disappointed Saez recently announced that due to the shortage of suckers … oops I mean investors, his banana project will probably never get off the ground.

You are probably thinking to yourself, "Well at least now that his project is scrapped, Saez will return the $55,000 to the Canada Council."

Ha. Clearly you don't know very much about art.

When it comes to Canada Council grants there are no refunds.

Flying banana or no flying banana, Saez gets to keep the government money.

When asked about this failed banana investment, Carole Breton, of the Canada Council, explained, "We understand that sometimes, for all sorts of reasons, there is no creation at the end ... this is money for research, not for results."

Isn't it good to know the people responsible for handing out our tax dollars don't expect results?

Still, maybe Breton has a point about the importance of funding this sort of "research."

Just imagine all the practical applications that could arise through using tax dollars to research giant flying bananas.

Perhaps, for example, the Canadian Air Force could use such information to assemble an elite squadron of "Airborne Attack Bananas."

We could then deploy them above Afghanistan to strike fear into the hearts of our enemies:

Taliban No. 1: Oh no, the Canadians are sending gigantic flying bananas against us. All is lost. We must surrender.

Taliban No. 2: Curses to the Canada Council for providing the necessary funds for flying banana research.

To be fair, not all the grants the Canada Council dishes out are goofy.

Some are downright insane.

For instance, the council once awarded $15,000 to "shock artist" Istvan Kantor, whose chief claim to fame was that he liked to walk into museums and splatter blood on priceless pieces of art.

It gives a whole new meaning to the phrase "blood money."

Of course, maybe we need the Canada Council to subsidize artists such as Kantor and

Saez with our tax dollars.

And maybe the majority of Canadians support these subsidies because they ensure our artistic community remains vibrant and creative.

Yeah, sure and maybe bananas can fly.

(Originally appeared in the Sun Media *Chain, August 5, 2008)*

Making Polar Bears Cry

David Suzuki preaches that setting our air conditioners just a few degrees higher will make a big difference for our environment.

And he's absolutely right.

I set my air conditioner a few degrees higher recently and my environment was changed so much I felt like a piece of bacon frying in Satan's kitchen.

Dying of heat stroke, of course, is just one of the "little things" we are supposed to do to help stave off Texas-sized hurricanes, melting glaciers and Al Gore documentaries.

In the name of saving the planet, environmentalists have all sorts of other lifestyle-altering tips such as "Instead of driving your car, why not turn it into a giant organic composter."

And when environmentalists are not nagging us with these "helpful hints" they are trying to make us feel guilty, albeit with scientifically based arguments like: "Do as we say or else polar bears will cry."

Still, environmentalists aren't the only ones out to change our lifestyles. So are politicians.

Take Prime Minister Stephen Harper's brilliant "green plan" to save the planet.

In case you haven't heard about it, Harper's plan seems based on a single premise: The world has too much food.

So to cut this dangerous surplus, the PM is courageously spending $1.5 billion on a scheme to turn crops into gasoline.

And already his plan is having an impact; today people worldwide are less concerned about global warming; unfortunately they are now more concerned about global starving.

Way to go Stephen.

Then there's Liberal leader Stéphane Dion's plan to impose a "carbon tax."

Whereas Harper's green plan will make us hungrier, Dion's will make us poorer.

Actually, that's unfair.

Dion's proposed carbon tax is "revenue neutral" meaning it will just make Alberta poorer.

This might upset Albertans, but Dion is operating according to a sophisticated economic model. For the non-economist layman this model can be simplified thusly: "Alberta never votes Liberal, so who cares?"

Besides, despite its drawbacks, Dion's plan will help avert a climate change catastrophe, right?

Wrong. It won't. And neither will Harper's plan and nor will all those little lifestyle altering tips environmental activists like to dish out.

Why do I say that?

Well, first of all the climate crisis will never go away because the environmental lobby won't let it go away.

The day will never come when Suzuki will go on national television and say: "Hey guess what? Because so many Canadians bought energy-efficient popcorn makers, the world is saved from ecological disaster. Good work everybody. I will now close down my foundation, relinquish my fame and vanish into obscurity."

If anything, "green" pressure groups have an incentive to exaggerate the world's environmental problems – and they do.

Secondly, if global warming is real and if human industrial activity is to blame, the only real cure would be for the whole world to revert to a pre-Fred Flinstone level of technology. Yabba dabba doo!

So that's why we shouldn't let environmental fanatics or politicians lay a guilt trip on us.

Let's just enjoy life as happily and comfortably as possible.

Idle your car in a Tim Hortons drive-through, don't throw out your old beer fridge, keep granny's dialysis machine plugged in.

The polar bears won't mind.

Now excuse me, I need to turn my air conditioner down a few degrees.

(Originally appeared in the Sun Media *Chain July 17, 2008)*

Union leaders finally see the dangers of gag laws

Seven British Columbia unions and the B.C. Federation of Labour will soon be in court to challenge Premier Gordon Campbell's Bill 42, an "election gag law" which infringes on every British Columbian's right to free political speech.

And all I can say to the union leaders involved in this important fight is: What the heck took you guys so long?

After all, Premier Campbell isn't the first politician to stifle free political expression. More than eight years ago former Prime Minister Jean Chrétien enacted a federal election gag law quite similar to Campbell's Bill 42.

In fact, the two gag laws are nearly identical.

Both gag laws impose severe restrictions on how much money citizens and independent organizations can spend on "political advertising", both have broad and vague definitions as to what constitutes "political advertising" and both laws give politicians and political parties a virtual monopoly on election debate.

I know all about Chrétien's gag law, because the group I used to work for – the National Citizens Coalition – challenged it in the courts.

The NCC believed Chrétien's gag law was undemocratic.

We believed that in a true democracy all citizens – not just politicians – should have the right to freely exchange ideas and opinions during elections.

Our view was simple: Democracies work best when there is a free unregulated, marketplace of ideas; the more opinions which get expressed, the more views voters are exposed to, the better.

That's why we opposed any attempt by governments to thwart free election speech, which we argued was a core democratic freedom guaranteed in the Charter of Rights and Freedoms.

And although the NCC was a small "c" conservative organization, we did not see this fight as one pitting Right vs. Left.

That's because Chrétien's gag law is blind to ideology; it silences all citizens and groups regardless of their political slant.

In the next federal election, for instance, pro-gay rights groups, environmental organizations, gun control activists, anti-poverty advocates will all be banned from effectively speaking out and promoting their agendas.

Yet, by and large, the left-wing in this country actually supported Chrétien's gag law.

Strangely, they did not see it as an infringement on free speech, but rather as a necessary "reform" to stop the "rich" and "well-heeled" from "buying elections."

Union bosses bought into this argument as well.

Commenting in one of its newsletters on the NCC's battle against gag laws, the National Union of Public and General Employees wrote:

"The NCC masquerades as a grassroots organization but it is basically a secretively-run front for corporate causes. It has long campaigned for the untrammeled right of big business to influence the electoral process by funding special-interest campaigns."

And so, no major left-wing group, no "progressive" activist, no union boss supported the NCC in its fight to defend the right to free political speech.

In 2004 we took our case to the Supreme Court of Canada, virtually alone – and we lost. In a 6-3 ruling the Supreme Court justices upheld the gag law as constitutional.

Would that ruling have been any different had say a few prominent union leaders joined our legal challenge to Chrétien's gag law?

Who knows?

All we do know is that the Supreme Court's ruling paved the way for Premier Campbell to introduce his own version of the gag law.

Of course, it's no secret as to why Campbell went the gag law route. He wants a gag law for the same reason

Chrétien wanted one: To shut down the voices of people who oppose his government, which in the case of Premier Campbell means union bosses.

In other words, it's now the unions who are being cast as the "rich" "well heeled special interests" who want to "buy elections." And so now that the gag is on the other mouth so to speak, union bosses are finally waking up the importance of free speech.

As Angela Schira, secretary-treasurer of the B.C. federation of Labour recently told the media that Campbell's "gag law really isn't enhancing any democracy. It's silencing critics, or people who may speak out about government issues."

Where were you Ms. Schira when the NCC needed you? At any rate, I wish the B.C. unions all the luck in the world with their court challenge.

But unfortunately, this is a classic case of doing too little, too late.

(Originally appeared in the Vancouver Sun *July 4, 2008)*

Disarm the Gun Hobbyists

Ask the average person on the street for his or her view on hobbies and you would probably hear something to the effect that they are fun and harmless activities.

Ha. Shows you what the average person knows.

Toronto Mayor David Miller, who doesn't care what average people think (unless it's an average person who leads a public sector union), knows the awful, horrible truth about these so-called harmless activities.

Sometimes hobbies go bad and kill.

A case in point is any hobby that includes the use of a gun.

As Miller recently explained, such hobbies as target shooting, gun collecting and competitive shooting are actually so dangerous they could destroy western civilization as we know it.

Well, OK, he didn't exactly put it that way.

What he did say is that gun hobbies directly result "in people being shot to death on the streets of Toronto."

In other words, guns don't kill people; gun hobbies do.

That's why Miller wants to make it illegal to own any kind of gun for any kind of purpose or hobby.

Now, of course, I expect the usual "gun lover" crowd will be all up in arms (so to speak) about Miller's anti-gun plan.

They will say Miller is engaging in typical left-wing, over-the-top rhetoric.

But let's consider the facts.

Fact one: target shooting is an Olympic event. To qualify for this Olympic event requires that a) you own a pistol and b) you do lots of practice shooting stuff.

Clearly this is a deadly combination.

Just imagine what would happen if crazed Olympians started patrolling our streets taking pot-shots at passersby just so they could increase their skill level.

Yeah, sure it might help them win a gold medal and make us all proud to be Canadian, but just consider the cost in human life!

Fact two: many of the guns people collect are actually antiques. If the popularity of programs like the *Antiques Road Show* has taught us anything it's that the retro look is definitely in style these days.

And if there's one thing your typical gun wielding criminal cares about, it's style.

Surely no self-respecting thug would go for a modern imported American hand gun, when he could dazzle his fellow gang members with a stylish Civil War-era Colt revolver.

So no doubt criminals are ransacking homes across the city to get their hands on classic weapons.

Although I don't have the actual statistics in front of me, it wouldn't surprise me a bit if an inordinate number of shootings in Toronto over the past few years involved muzzle-loading muskets.

Fact three: Gun owners typically like to shoot in special firing ranges. We have all seen these ranges on countless TV cop shows. The hero inevitably squeezes off a few rounds right into the heart of a black silhouette paper target. Seems safe right?

Wrong.

What would happen if say a group of school children happened to wander into one of these target ranges? And what if from a distance they happened to look like black silhouettes?

Carnage would ensue.

So considering all these facts, Torontonians should absolutely support Mayor Miller in his crusade to ensure gun hobbyists are disarmed.

Of course, Toronto's criminals would still be armed to the teeth.

But that's OK because when they shoot people it's not a hobby; it's more like a job.

(Originally appeared in the Western Standard Online Magazine *June 6, 2008)*

The bureaucrats who work at Elections Canada don't get angry, they get even.

And that explains why Elections Canada officials ordered that highly publicized "raid" this week of Conservative Party headquarters.

That raid was not so much about investigating a possible breach of election laws, as it was about settling an old score.

To be blunt, Elections Canada bureaucrats and Prime Minister Stephen Harper have been engaged in an eight-year-long blood feud. The bureaucrats don't like him, and he in turn doesn't like them.

The bad feelings started back when Harper was still president of the National Citizens Coalition. The NCC at the time was waging a constitutional war against the federal government's election gag laws.

These are laws which place severe restrictions on how much money private citizens or groups can spend on "election advertising." In Harper's view, these laws infringed on free expression.

Then Chief Electoral Officer Jean-Pierre Kingsley had a different view. He was a vocal proponent of gag laws and had vigorously lobbied the government to enact the legal restrictions on free speech.

So for us at the NCC, the officials at Elections Canada were not just disinterested bureaucrats; they were the enemy.

And we didn't pull any punches in criticizing Elections Canada officials over this issue.

Harper was especially critical of the overzealous and heavy-handed tactics Elections Canada used to enforce the gag laws.

For instance, he was particularly angry at the way the agency used its powers to bully Paul Bryan, a British Columbia software developer, who on election night 2000 posted real-time Atlantic Canada elections results on his website while the polls were still open in BC.

This violated section 329 of the Canada Elections Act, which bans the "premature transmission" of election results.

Now Bryan wasn't the only person who prematurely posted voting information. Yahoo! Canada, ABCnews.com and various other websites were also posting election results.

But only Bryan was charged. Elections Canada dispatched the police to raid his home, where they seized two of his computer hard drives.

The NCC saw this as an injustice and we took up Bryan's cause.

To explain why we were doing so, Harper, in a letter written to the NCC supporters, declared, "The jackasses at Elections Canada are out of control." He also called Kingsley a "dangerous man" who was using "iron-fisted bully tactics."

Yes, these were tough words, but they were also accurate.

How did Elections Canada react? Well the jackasses kicked back.

Late in 2001 Election Canada charged the NCC with violating the election gag law. Our supposed crime was that we ran 15-second TV ads in the 2000 federal election which had condemned, ironically enough, the election gag law.

The charge was a sham.

The NCC TV ad was not election advertising. It didn't tell anybody who to vote for and it didn't support or oppose any political party. We were simply trying to raise funds for a constitutional court challenge.

Nevertheless, the NCC was forced to defend itself in a long and costly criminal court proceeding.

This was simply a case of Elections Canada bureaucrats punishing us for opposing the gag law and for opposing them.

It wasn't a prosecution; it was a persecution.

And interestingly, the charge against the NCC was laid just a few weeks before Harper announced he was running for the leadership of the Canadian Alliance.

Coincidence?

So when I see RCMP officers executing a "raid" or if you prefer a "visit" to Tory offices, on behalf of Elections Canada, with the media and Liberal camera people in tow, I get a strong sense of déjà vu.

Was this raid a case of justice in action, or simply an example of bureaucrats acting out a grudge against a man who used to be such a thorn in their collective side?

There is no question the optics for the Conservatives on this question are bad. They may yet win in the court of law, but they have been badly hurt in the court of public opinion.

It looks like the jackasses at Elections Canada are out of control – again.

(Gerry Nicholls is the former vice president of the National Citizens Coalition. www.gerrynicholls.com)

(This article originally appeared in the National Post *April 18, 2008)*

Is Dion Getting Delusional

Not being a psychologist maybe I shouldn't say what I am about to say.

But it seems to me the federal Liberals are suffering from some sort of collective delusional disorder.

How else to explain the recent madcap utterances of Liberal Leader Stéphane Dion and assorted other Liberal MPs about how they are ready and willing to force a federal election this fall?

Talk about being out of touch with political reality.

I mean let's be honest. The Dion-led Liberals have about as much chance of winning an election this fall as John Edwards has of being named Husband of the Year.

Yet – and here's the real delusional part – some Liberals actually believe the popularity of American Democratic presidential nominee Barack Obama will somehow carry over to Stéphane Dion and help lead him to victory.

As one unnamed Liberal MP recently told the media: "The sweet spot for calling a general election would be late November ... so you give people a little bit of an effect of the afterglow of hope and change with Obama."

Good theory.

But here's the less than sweet spot reality: Stéphane Dion is no Barack Obama.

In fact, comparing Dion to Obama is like comparing a firecracker to an atom bomb or like comparing the CBC comedy *Royal Canadian Air Farce* to some other TV comedy that's actually funny.

One obvious difference between the two men is charisma. Obama is so jam-packed with charisma it's practically seeping out of his ears. Dion, on the other hand, not only has no charisma he actually emits rays of "anti-charisma," which have been known to repel voters over a five-km radius.

That's why Obama and Dion must never meet.

If *Star Trek* has taught me anything, it's that if Obama's charisma were ever came into direct contact with Dion's anti-charisma, it would mean the total annihilation of our universe.

The other big difference between Dion and Obama is that Obama actually understands how politics works.

He understands, for instance, that to win an election a politician must stay away from complicated policy ideas.

Hence, Obama's election strategy is so simple it can be summed up in a single sentence:

"Vote for me because I am not George Bush."

Dion, by contrast, has decided to pin his election hopes on persuading Canadians of the merits of his "Green Shift" scheme, a plan so convoluted even Stephen Hawking couldn't figure it out.

How convoluted is Dion's Green Shift plan?

Well let's put it this way, in the time it would take Dion

to properly explain it to you, global warming would have melted three more glaciers.

None of this is to suggest Dion can't copy some of Obama's tactics.

Obama, for example, recently had a successful international tour which included a speech before a massive and adoring crowd in Berlin.

It would be a great idea for Dion to follow Obama's lead and hop on the next plane to Europe.

Of course, even if he were naked and standing atop the Eiffel Tower, Dion would never draw any kind of crowd overseas.

But that's not the point.

The point is Dion would be far away and the farther away he is from Canadian voters, the better it would be for the Liberal Party.

And that's no delusion.

(Originally appeared in the Sun Media *Chain – August 14, 2008)*

DION HAS A DEBT DILEMMA

Liberal leader Stéphane Dion wants to fight the next federal election on the environment. And for good reason.

Better Canadians focus on his green plan, than on his red ink. The fact is Dion faces a personal debt – left over from his leadership campaign – of about $600,000.

Being debt-ridden isn't exactly a selling point for a guy who wants to run the country's finances.

To make matters worse, Dion has more operating costs than other party leaders; other leaders, for instance, don't require language experts to translate their English speeches into English.

Eliminating Dion's debt, however, won't be easy for one simple reason: The Liberals are bad fundraisers. Consider in the first quarter of this year the Liberals raised just $850,000 compared with the $5 million the Conservatives raised and the $1.1 million the NDP raked in.

Finishing behind the Tories is bad enough, but to place second to the NDP in fundraising is really embarrassing; it's like losing a congeniality contest to Simon Cowell. Of course, it wasn't always hard for the Liberals to raise money. In fact, back in the days when Jean Chretien was running the Liberal party, fundraising was an easy three-step process:

Step 1. Have Chretien contact key Liberal supporters – "key" in the sense that they are CEOs of massive corporate conglomerates.

Step 2. Have Chretien ask the CEOs for a contribution.

Step 3. Have Chretien and the Liberals cash cheques worth about a gazillion dollars.

This money then was used to buy TV ads warning voters about how the Conservatives were "the party of the rich." However, thanks to new campaign finance laws, corporations can no longer give donations to political parties and individual political contributions are limited to about $1,000 a year.

Consequently, political parties must now rely on smaller, grassroots donations.

This is bad news for the Liberals since the only grassroots they know about are the kind you find on the golf course. Hence their lack of fundraising success.

A typical Liberal fundraising letter might look a little like this:

"Dear Canadian: As you know, the Liberal party is out of power. That's unacceptable. We Liberals must rule. It's our right. So send us your cash now! We know you can afford it. Just buy less popcorn and beer. Signed Stéphane Dion."

Needless to say no one would respond to a letter like that. Well, OK nobody except maybe the CBC.

Still to their credit, the Liberals are said to be trying new and innovative fundraising techniques. Indeed here are some of the ideas they are reportedly considering:

- Turning Stornoway, Dion's official residence, into a bed and breakfast. Guests will get guided tours of famous Liberal landmarks, such as the restaurant where the first Adscam scheme was hatched.

- Broadcasting a special cable pay-per-view "mixed martial arts" bout, pitting Michael "The Professor" Ignatieff against Bob "The Economy Killer" Rae.

- Negotiating "product placement" sponsorship deals wherein Dion would sip a Coke or bite into a Big Mac before he asks a question in the House of Commons.

Maybe these money-raising concepts will work. Or maybe not.

Perhaps during the next federal election a cash-strapped Dion will be forced to cancel his campaign jet and rely instead on hitchhiking and public transit.

At least he could say he's doing it for the environment.

(Originally appeared in the Sun Media *chain July 31, 2008)*

IS Canada a left-wing country?

One of the myths about Canada is that it's a left-wing country.

According to this myth conservatism – with its emphasis on limited government, free markets and individual freedom – just won't sell here, it's too alien a concept for Canadians to accept.

Big government socialism, on the other hand, is supposed to be as Canadian as maple syrup. Socialism is supposed to define us a nation. It's who we are. Even some conservatives buy into this argument. In his book, *ß*, Tom Flanagan, who was formerly a campaign manager for the Conservative Party, writes "Canada is not yet a conservative or Conservative country. We can't win votes if we veer too far to the right of the median voter."

If this was true, of course, if Canada really was a socialist country, those of us who believe in conservative ideals should simply give up. Trying to sell conservatism would be a waste of time.

The smart thing to do would be to join the Liberal Party and wait for slush fund kickbacks. But is Canada really a left wing country? For much of our history that certainly wasn't the case. As William Watson documents in his book Globalization and the Meaning of Canadian Life, for much of our history government power in Canada was more limited and less interventionist than the American government.

Watson notes, for instance, Americans started collecting income tax in 1913, while Canada didn't introduce such a tax until 1917. Our policy of subsidizing railway construction was actually a copy of a previous American policy. And while Canada did eventually duplicate elements of the American New Deal programs during the depression, our version of the New Deal was more cautious.

If anything Canada's tradition was one of private initiative and individual liberty. Of course, that all came to a halt in the late 1960s with the coming of the Pierre Trudeau dynasty. Rather than building on Canada's past traditions, Trudeau triggered a social and political revolution that degraded our heritage and overturned our historic values.

At that point, Canada did indeed begin to drift into socialist waters – with a devastating result for our economy. Trudeau's interventionist policies, his expansion of government, his fiscally irresponsible measures left a legacy of high taxes, gigantic national debt and bloated bureaucracies.

Yet, ironically while Trudeau's economic policies were dismal failures, his political revolution was a total success. His left-wing vision of Canada became, in essence, the unofficial orthodoxy of the country's political establishment. Anyone who challenged this orthodoxy, anyone who promoted the idea of free enterprise or individual freedom or less government (all of them traditional Canadian values) was deemed outside the political mainstream, or worse – labeled an extremist. This is what created the illusion that Canada was a "left-wing country." And it is an illusion.

There is a definite disconnect between the left-leaning views of our establishment and the views of the Canadian population as a whole. And this disconnect explains why Canadian conservatives managed to achieve important victories in the last few decades. True blue conservative Mike Harris won back to back majorities governments in Ontario; Preston Manning created the conservative/populist Reform Party; Brian Mulroney enacted a free trade agreement.

The Liberal Party, under Jean Chrétien, balanced the budget.

The conservative-leaning ADQ has emerged as a political force in Quebec. What's more, after they occurred, conservative successes became mainstream. Even the Liberal Party, for instance, now supports free trade. Balanced budgets are almost mandatory for governments. And no one talks anymore about nationalizing our industries. So much for Canada being a left wing country!

(Originally appeared in Report Magazine *November, 2007)*

JACK MEET HUGO

NDP leader Jack Layton must be a little envious of Venezuela's socialist boss Hugo Chavez.

Chavez, after all, is currently the hip and happening star of the world's radical, chic left-wing crowd.

That status became official, by the way, when American actor and left-wing activist Sean Penn recently paid the South American leader a visit.

When Hollywood celebrities start hanging around a leader, it's the official stamp of "politically trendy" approval.

Sorry Castro, your Cuban-style retro-1950s Stalinism is out. Hugo Chavez is in.

Chavez – undaunted by socialism's unbroken record of failure – is zealously and unabashedly taking the teachings of Marx and Lenin out of the university classrooms and putting them into practice.

In fact, he has hammered Venezuela's private sector with wide-scale property expropriations, nationalizations, price fixing and currency controls. (Kind of sounds like Canada in the 1970s.)

Meanwhile, while Chavez boasts about "breaking the chains of the old exploitive capitalist system," what is Jack Layton doing here in Canada for the socialist cause?

Well he is pushing hard to regulate bank fees for ATMs.

Not all that exciting is it?

Hardly the kind of revolutionary action needed to mobilize the proletariat, let alone get you invited to posh Hollywood parties.

So who knows, maybe in an attempt to boost his socialist cachet, Layton will undergo a left wing makeover. Maybe he will even adopt the Chavez model as NDP policy.

Just imagine if he did that.

And further imagine what would happen if a Chavez-inspired Layton ever got himself elected Prime Minister. (OK, I know Layton becoming Prime Minister is about as likely as Michael Vick starring in the next Lassie movie, but work with me here.)

What would a Chavez-style revolution mean for Canada?

Well, for one thing, Layton might adopt Chavez's "progressive, left wing" stance regarding the media. And Chavez's "progressive left wing stance" was to recently shut down an independent TV station that dared to criticize him and replace it with what he called "socialist television."

But come to think to think of it, that won't work here. Canada already has "socialist television." It's called the CBC.

OK so maybe a Prime Minister Layton would adopt another Chavez policy which was to force the Venezuelan armed forces to adopt the motto "Fatherland, socialism or death."

Catchy, isn't it?

But on second thought, I am pretty sure that slogan is already taken. Isn't it inscribed on the coat of arms of the Supreme Court of Canada? So that's out.

Well there is one other Chavez policy a Prime Minister Layton could possibly emulate. Chavez recently announced sweeping changes to the country's constitution that would give him dictatorial powers.

Some observers have called this move undemocratic; Chavez, however, calls it a "transfer of power to the people."

Maybe a Prime Minister Layton could arrange for a similar "transfer." Oops, I forgot. In Canada prime ministers already have close to dictatorial powers.

So Layton clearly has a problem when it comes to winning the adulation of the Sean Penns of the world.

Simply put, he can't really trigger a socialist revolution in this country.

Why? Because somebody has already beaten him to it.

(Originally appeared in the Sun Media *chain, August 27, 2007)*

It seems Canada's "linguist duality" needs a tune-up.

Or so thinks Prime Minister Stephen Harper, who recently dispatched former New Brunswick premier Bernard Lord on a cross-country tour to "review the state of bilingualism" in Canada.

Lord, of course, is perfect for this role. He is fluently bilingual, he's known as a "consensus builder" and he's a failed Conservative politician who could use the work.

Armed with these credentials, Lord will consult with minority language groups and produce a report which will likely recommend doling out money to minority language groups.

It's all pretty predictable.

A more interesting idea would have been to send Lord out on a cross-country tour to ask this question: Does anyone even care about Trudeau-style official bilingualism anymore?

Quebeckers, at least, would probably answer no.

After all, Quebec is actively promoting state-sanctioned unilingualism. In fact, thanks to its draconian language laws, enforced by draconian language police, English has the same status in Quebec as teddy bears named Muhammad have in the Sudan.

But what about the rest of Canada? Do Canadians outside of Quebec care about embracing the spirit of official bilingualism?

The statistics say no.

According to 2006 census information, about nine per cent of Canadian anglophones reported they could converse in both languages. Plus, if you consider only bilingual anglophones outside Quebec, that number falls to a little more than seven per cent.

And even that low figure probably overstates the case because the census question only asked respondents if they could speak French "well enough to conduct a conversation."

In other words, a lot of these "bilingual" anglophones would probably be hard pressed to continue a French conversation much beyond, "Bonjour, comment ca va?" or "Je fait du ski."

If anglo-Canadians cared about bilingualism, wouldn't it follow that more of them would make an effort to learn French, beyond what they were forced to learn in high school?

What's more, fewer young anglophones are learning to speak French. According to the report, the bilingualism rate for Canadians in the 15 to 19 age range has dropped from 16 to 13 per cent in the past 10 years.

And those young people who are bilingual seem to be losing the ability to speak French over time. In 2001, 14.7 per cent of anglophones aged 15 to 19 were bilingual. In 2006, however, only 12.2 per cent of that same cohort reported being bilingual.

Use it or lose it, indeed.

OK, I know it's sacrilege to suggest official bilingualism isn't working. But facts are facts.

The reality is that, outside of New Brunswick and parts of eastern Ontario, Canada is an overwhelmingly unilingual English-speaking country that includes a large French-speaking region, i.e. Quebec.

And here's another reality: a growing number of Canadians who are bilingual don't speak English and French, they speak English and Mandarin, or English and Portuguese, or English and Arabic, as a trip in any taxi cab will quickly prove.

Even the Liberal party seems to be paying only lip service to the bilingual ideal.

How else do you explain their picking Stéphane Dion as leader, a man who speaks French and a language that only bears a slight resemblance to English?

So isn't it time we all stopped pretending Canada is a bilingual country? And more to the point, isn't it time government officials realized they are out of sync with Canadians?

Canadians care about fixing our health care system, the environment and national security. What they don't care about is a language policy developed in the 1960s. But try telling that to the Ottawa political establishment.

C'est impossible.

(Originally appeared in the Windsor Star, *January 8, 2008)*

Acknowledgements

I can honestly say this is the best book I have ever written. But then again, it's the only book I have ever written. And its publication would not have been possible without the help and support of many people.

First, I want to thank my former colleagues from the National Citizens Coalition, especially Alex Alvaro, Sue Schuhmacher, Jeff Ball, Jane Lee, Mark Poole, Laura Watson, Colin T. Brown, Elizabeth Robertson, Heather Fellows, Ken Wakeman, David Somerville, John McLaughlin, Arthur Finkelstein and the late Ken McDonald. We were quite a team.

Next, I would like to thank Patti Nicholls, Rondi Adamson, Paul Tuns and Michael Nicholls for reading all or important parts of the manuscript. I am grateful to all of them for their support and encouragement.

I would also like to thank my editor for helping me look like a better writer and my publisher, Tristan Emmanuel of Freedom Press, who approached me with the idea of writing this story and whose enthusiasm for the project never wavered.

211

And I want to express my gratitude to the friends I've made since leaving the NCC, people whose principles and values have inspired me to keep up the fight for freedom. That list includes Ed Barr, John Dobson, John Gray, Patrick Basham, Bryan Bennett, Greg Radovich, Steve Lafleur, Jonathan Fortier, Roy Eappen, Peter Jaworski, Matt Bufton, Janet Neilson, Theo Caldwell, Adrian Redmond, Paul Synott and from the Oakville Mafia, Viggo Lewis, Jack Lewis and Wilf Rudd.

Other friends I would like to acknowledge for being there when I needed someone to bounce ideas off include Claudia Hepburn, Mike Druhan, Joseph Ben-Ami, Adrienne Batra, John Capobianco, Howard Galganov, Peter Holle, John Robson, Charlie Conn, John Carpay, Avril Allen, Derek Nelson, Michel Kelly-Gagnon, Kevin Gaudet, Kim McConnell, David Gratzer, Phil Green, Malkin Dare, Doretta Wilson, Claire Joly, Kennedy Hong, Russ Kuykendall, Bob Michener, Linda Leatherdale, Pierre Lemieux, Brent Tyler, John Williamson, Rebecca Walberg, John Mortimer, Clinton Desveaux, Jason Clemens, Kirk West, Terence Corcoran, Naresh Ragubeer, Claire Hoy, Neil Seeman, Rolph Penner, Karen Selick, Marnee and Stephen Stern, Craig Shirley, John Thompson and David Frum.

Thanks also to the editors and producers who gave me a chance to hone my arguments in their opinion pages or on the air: Marni Soupcoff, Jonathan Kay, Sarah Thomson, Justine Connelly, Rob Breakenridge, Rodney Deiztman, Jay Lafayette, John Wilson, John Coleman, Fazil Mihlar,

Licia Corbella, Charles Adler, Natasha Hassan, Michael Coren, Michael Zweip and Rob Granatstein.

And of course, special thanks must lovingly go to my wife Patti and to my sons Nolan and Tommy, who endured, throughout the process of writing this book, my cranky demands for quiet and my intolerably messy work space.

Finally, I must thank the man who set the standard for personal integrity and courage: the late Colin M. Brown.

I am very grateful to all of the above.

1 Kenneth McDonald, *A Wind of the Heath: A Memoir*, (Epic Press, 2003), 243-244

2 Colin Brown, "CMB Twenty Years On," *National Citizens Review*, 3 June 2007: 2-3

3 Brooke Jeffrey, *Hard Right Turn: The New Face of Neo-Conservatism in Canada*, (Harper Collins, 1999) 408

4 David Somerville, address to conference of the International 6 Society for Individual Liberty, Whistler, B.C. August 1996

5 Ariel Kaminer, Larissa MacFarquhar, Liesl Schillinger, "The 100 Smartest New Yorkers," *New York Magazine* January 30, 1995: 42

6 Bob Rae, *From Protest to Power: Personal Reflections on a Life in Politics*, (Viking, 1996) 196

7 "Harper claims National Citizens Coalition was self-owned and operated business," Liberal Party news release, September 15, 2008

8 Robert Macdermid & Fred Fletcher, *Advocacy Groups and the Ad War*, 1999

9 Murray Dobbin, "Will the real Stephen Harper please stand up?" *The Straight Goods*, January 2006

10 Jeffrey, *Hard Right Turn*, 415

11 "Hargrove attacks Harper as separatist," *National Post*, January 18, 2006

12 "Harper claims National Citizens Coalition was self-owned an operated business." September 15, 2008

13 Scott Feschuk, "Harper rejects run at Tory leadership," *Globe and Mail*, April 10, 1998

14 Peter Menzies, "Harper making Reform blood boil," *Calgary Herald*, April 27, 1998

15 Stephen Harper, "Why I hate gag laws," *Globe and Mail*, June 13, 2000

16 "Property Rights Denied by Court," *Conservative Times*, April 1999

17 "Language Law Decision in Quebec," *Maclean's*, November 1999

18 Francois Cardinal, "De l'argent Canadian contre la Loi 101," *Le Devoir*, June 23, 2000

19 Warren Kinsella, *Kicking Ass in Canadian Politics*, (Random House, 2001) 5

20 Stephen Harper, "Leaders and Regions," *Globe and Mail*, November 14, 2000

21 Brian Laghi, "UA plan has Reformers evenly split, survey says," *Globe and Mail*, January 26, 2000

22 Ibid.

23 Sheldon Alberts, "Harper mounts campaign to lead the right: Behind the scenes," *National Post*, June 30, 2001

24 Tom Flanagan, *Harper's Team: Behind the Scenes in the Conservatives Rise to Power*, (McGill-Queens University Press, 2007) 47

25 Ibid, 48

26 Ibid, 48

27 "War of words picks up in Alliance race," *Globe and Mail*, February 9, 2002

28 Stephen Harper, "Three tips for the CA: policy, policy and policy," *Freedom Watch*, 2001

29 Stephen Harper, "Reform MP speaks at NCC dinner," *Consensus*, June 1994

30 Gerry Nicholls, "Steer clear of Liberal lite," *National Post* March 11, 2005

31 Gerry Nicholls, "Fresh Start for Canada," *Windsor Star*, January 27, 2006

32 Stephen Harper, "Questioning income trusts puts seniors at risk," *National Post*, October 26, 2005

33 Gerry Nicholls, "Spending spree hypocrisy," *Globe and Mail*, March 15, 2007

34 Andrew Coyne, "Flaherty biggest of the big spenders," *National Post*, March 20, 2007

35 Jason Clemons, Niels Veldhuis, "Conservative budget in name Only," *Vancouver Sun*, March 20, 2007

36 Gerry Nicholls, "Aren't Tories about lower taxes?" *Toronto Sun*, March 26, 2007

37 Gerry Nicholls, "Costly Harper win," *National Post*, March 28, 2007

38 Tonda MacCharles, "Harper critic loses lobby group job," *Toronto Star*, April 5, 2007

39 "Time to Move On," http://nationalcitizens.ca/blog/2007/04/05/time-to-move-on/

40 "Budget 2007", *Freedom Watch*, April 2007

41 "It's the economy, stupid," http://nationalcitizens.ca/blog/2008/10/06/its-the-economy-stupid/

42 Nigel Hannaford, "Tribalism marks voting patterns," *Calgary Herald*, November 3, 2007

43 Brian Laghi, "Fired NCC official accuses Harper of betraying his roots," *Globe and Mail*, April 12, 2007

44 Flanagan, *Harper's Team*, 279

45 Ibid. 278

46 "PM announces tougher food and product safety legislation to protect Canadian consumers," Conservative Party News release, April 8, 2008

47 Andrew Coyne, "The Harper leadership cult," *Maclean's*, September 10, 2008

48 Paul Tuns, "Harper's real 'hidden agenda'," *The Interim*, November 2008

49 Rondi Adamson, "A Political Ruckus … in Canada?!" *Christian Science Monitor*, December 10, 2008

50 Joseph Ben-Ami, "Conservatives: Stop Whining and get into the game," *Ottawa Citizen*, October 11, 2008

51 "Insurgent Republicans The Club for Growth wants to create a free market GOP, whether the party likes it or not," *Reason Magazine*, December 2006

Gerry Nicholls is one of Canada's most prominent defenders of our economic and political freedoms. For more than twenty years he was a senior officer at the National Citizens Coalition, Canada's largest independent pro-free market advocacy group. He currently works as a freelance writer and as an independent political consultant. His columns on political affairs have appeared in several national and major regional newspapers including the *National Post*, the *Globe and Mail*, and the Sun Media chain.

Gerry is also a Senior Fellow with the Democracy Institute and serves as a director for the Institute for Liberal Studies and the Society for Quality Education. He currently resides in Oakville with his wife and two children. You can learn more about Gerry at his website www.gerrynicholls.com

FR€∃DOM PRESS
CANADA INC.

Conservative Books
Written by Canadians
For Canadians

www.freedompress.ca

Business History

Freedom Press has been in operation since 2003. Established initially as a self-publishing venture, Freedom Press quickly recognized the need to serve a specific segment of the Canadian book buying public.

Mission and Vision

Freedom Press is dedicated to producing, promoting and distributing excellent books by Canadian authors who write from a conservative and libertarian perspective. As a niche publisher, Freedom Press features Canadian authors whose message and ideology reflect Freedom Press's core principles: Free Speech and Freedom of Religion; Limited Government; Liberty through Law, Personal Responsibility, the Free Market, and Free Market Charity Initiatives; Individualism and Exceptionalism; and Positive Canadian Patriotism.

Description of Products and Services

A niche publisher since 2003, Freedom Press currently has 6 books in its catalogue. Although our authors range in their ideological commitments, all fall within the general framework of Freedom Press values. Our market strategy is to work with a client author (that is, someone who is a recognized leader/ writer/thinker within the conservative and libertarian camp) to showcase his or her work to the best advantage.

Key Features of the Products and Services

As a niche publisher that exclusively promotes conservative, libertarian authors who are Canadian and write for Canadians, Freedom Press has a unique mission and a particular advantage in developing a relatively untapped market. Conservatives and libertarians make up 35% of the voting public and are avid readers and buyers of books.

In evaluating the potential marketability of a client author, Freedom Press focuses on media exposure and an existing network of supporters and followers via web writings, print columns or monthly newsletters. The client author's public relations exposure is vital to the success of all publishing projects, because marketing and promotion will be directed at existing networks of supporters.

Future Products and Services

Freedom Press will continue to expand and diversify its roster of authors. In the next 5 years Freedom Press plans to publish 20 new authors and increase its catalogue to 50 – 70 excellent books. Freedom Press also plans to host yearly book launches that will highlight our writing talent. And Freedom Press will organize several conferences for its client authors and their networks of supporters.

Comparative Advantages in Production

Freedom Press's competitive advantage is simple: It is the only publisher focusing on a particular political market and seeking ways to serve that market's needs.

Current Catalogue

Jean Chretien: A Legacy of Scandal

Anyone interested in a serious examination of the Chretien years will benefit from Paul Tuns' *Jean Chretien: A Legacy Of Scandal*. Tuns' outstanding new book gives you the factual story behind the man, the party and the ten years of greed, power, corruption and scandal – from the many broken election promises like the G.S.T, to Shawinigate, APEC, Airbus, and finally Ad Scam, this book is a serious analysis for anyone interested in the hard facts. Paul Tuns truly leaves no stone unturned to get at our recent history.

Paul Tuns

Paul Tuns is a public affairs commentator and political analyst whose articles have appeared in more than 35 publications including the *National Post, Globe and Mail*, and the *Toronto Star*. He is the editor-in-chief of *The Interim*, Canada's life and family newspaper, and is a contributor to *Business Report*. He lives in Toronto with his wife and five children

Environmentalism and the Death of Science: Exposing the Lie of Eco-Religion

Environmentalism has become the leading religion in Canada and the Western world. It's a globalist ideology that is at war with science and at war with Christianity. This might be the only book published in North America that tackles the key religious components of modern Environmentalism, exposing their errors and demonstrating the incompatibility of orthodox Christianity and Environmentalism. In an era when Christian leaders, including the leadership of the National Association of Evangelicals, has embraced false notions such as cataclysmic climate change theory, this book is a timely antidote to such deception and ignorance.

Tim Bloedow

Timothy Bloedow has worked as a researcher, speech writer and media coordinator for two Members of Parliament in Canada's federal government. He is a writer and a real estate investor. He worked as a researcher and lobbyist for Campaign Life Coalition. Mr. Bloedow has run for office as a member of the Christian Heritage Party of Canada. He co-founded and published The Ottawa Times, a monthly newspaper, in the early 1990s. Mr. Bloedow has a Bachelor of Theology from Tyndale Bible College (then Ontario Bible College). He is married to Lynette and has two children, Ulyn and Daniel. He is motivated by a desire to explain and advance the comprehensive claims of Christ over every area of life.

Standing on Guard for Thee

This book is the antidote to those who would portray the Christian Right as a bunch of inarticulate Bible-thumpers, trying to impose their morality on everyone else. Michael Wagner proves, among other things, that Christianity was here first. And that, rather than being an "American import", Canada's Christian Right was a reaction to the secularist drive for influence in society, and an attempt to preserve what is best in Western culture.

Michael Wagner PhD

Michael is a freelance writer and homeschooling father with a BA (Honours) and MA in Political Science from the University of Calgary, and a PhD in Political Science from the University of Alberta. He makes his home in Edmonton with his wife and nine children.

The Great Canadian Comedy: From Laughter To Tears

Freedom of spoof and the right to levity are upheld and celebrated in this collection of 50 humour pieces.

Joe Campbell makes fun of doctors, lawyers, educators, literary critics, scientists, politicians, judges, royalty, journalists, comedians and hockey and football players, among others. He also takes aim at the Canadian Constitution, Dan Brown's Da Vinci Code, the uses and abuses of Christmas and Valentines Day, social engineering, gobbledygook and telephone chatter.

His treatment of the last two has given rise to Campbell's laws: 1) The volume of verbose writing varies directly with the ease of producing it; 2) The amount of idle chatter varies inversely with the cost of transmitting it.

Much of the time, though, Joe makes fun of himself, especially when he describes his encounters with writing, music, ballroom dancing, history and grammar, and his trying to learn a second language, being a temporary house husband, and growing old.

The humour ranges from farce to satire. The attitude is that of a somewhat bemused observer trying to make sense of the contradictions and incongruities of the world in which he lives.

Joe writes from the perspective of a small "c" conservative. Consequently, his satirical pieces are, no doubt, seen as politically incorrect and controversial.

Joe Campbell

Joe Campbell began producing humour in high school and published a few pieces after graduating from the University of Saskatchewan in arts and education. But distractions—earning a living, raising a family, leading a jazz band—sobered him up and he pronounced himself cured.

He spent ten years as a radio and television newsman, followed by 28 years as a "tame journalist" with his alma mater, handling media relations and various writing and editing chores.

Alas, after taking early retirement, he suffered a relapse into humour and some 130 of his light or satirical pieces have appeared in newspapers and magazines in Canada and the US.

Fifty of his previously published pieces are included in Take Me Out of the Ball Game, his first book of humour, which was shortlisted for the 2006 Stephen Leacock Memorial Medal for Humour.

Like writing, music has been an abiding interest. Joe took up the trumpet in high school, began playing with various bands and orchestras at age 15, and led the Joe Campbell Sextet in university. In 1967, he co-founded the Bridge City Dixieland Jazz Band, which was featured on radio and TV, on record, at Expo '86 in Vancouver, at the 1990 Chilliwack International Jazz Festival, and regularly at the SaskTel Saskatchewan Jazz Festival in Saskatoon, among a host of other events spanning more than a quarter of a century.

In retirement, he began concentrating on piano, in case his lungs give out before his fingers, and has performed publicly with another musician in what they call The Semi-Dynamic Duo.

Joe and his wife, Rosemary, live in Saskatoon, where they raised their nine children.

Christophobia: The Real Reason Behind Hate Crime Legislation

This book is about Bill C-250. Bill C-250 was known as "an Act to amend the Criminal Code of Canada (hate propaganda)." Actually, to be more precise, this book is about legal oppression. Bill C-250 represented the latest legislative initiative to silence moral disapproval of homosexuality. And ultimately, Bill C-250 is an attempt to suppress the Christian Gospel. The Bill was the legal face of a very real problem: Christophobia.

Warned: Canada's Revolution Against Faith, Family and Freedom Threatens America

 This book is essential reading for both Americans and Canadians even though it is more particularly directed to our American friends. Both countries face a serious challenge to their cultures. This book exposes the radical exploitation of Canada at the hands of extremist activists, leftwing politicians and a plethora of crusading activist judges, who are using their status in Canada to get at America. Their aim is marriage. But the prize is America. They want to use marriage as a weapon to systematically destroy the Judeo-Christian civilization of North America, but to do that they need America to "go gay". Gay "marriage" will open America up to the rest of the demands of the homosexual political movement. Everything from school curriculum to parental rights, adoption, the age of consent and religious freedoms will be up for grabs once gay "marriage" is made legal in America. Unless socons in both countries unite and work to resist these political opponents, we can kiss our continent good-bye.

To order any of these books go to:

www.freedompress.ca

Lightning Source Inc.
LaVergne, TN USA
14 August 2009
154915LV00007B/159/P